T0248397

DATES

Edible

Series Editor: Andrew F. Smith

EDIBLE is a revolutionary series of books dedicated to food and drink that explores the rich history of cuisine. Each book reveals the global history and culture of one type of food or beverage.

Already published

Dates

A Global History

Nawal Nasrallah

REAKTION BOOKS

Published by Reaktion Books Ltd
Unit 32, Waterside
44–48 Wharf Road
London N1 7UX, UK
www.reaktionbooks.co.uk

First published 2011
Copyright © Nawal Nasrallah 2011

Printed and bound in India by Replika Press Pvt. Ltd

A catalogue record for this book is available from the British Library

Nasrallah, Nawal.
Dates : a global history. – (Edible)
1. Dates (Fruit)
2. Date palm – History.
3. Date palm – social aspects.
4. Cooking (Dates)
I. Title II. Series
641.3 462-DC22

ISBN 978 1 86189 796 1

Contents

Introducing the Date

Palm-trees grow in great numbers over the whole of the flat
country, mostly of the kind which bears fruit, and this fruit
supplies them with bread, wine and honey.
Herodotus (484–425 BC), describing Babylonia

The date is a unique fruit, enjoyed in three states of ripeness.
When fully ripe but still firm, it is bright yellow or red, refresh-
ingly crunchy, juicy and moderately sweet. As it further ripens,
it gradually softens, starting from the top all the way down to
the calyx. The date looks partly firm and yellow or red, and
partly moist and brown and almost translucent. Then the
entire fruit becomes soft, loses its crunchiness and tastes even
sweeter and more succulent. If left on the tree to dry naturally
in the sun, its skin shrivels and darkens in hue. The date develops a scrumptious candy-like chewy texture. Technically, the
date can be labelled as fresh when eaten right after it has
been picked, but since it is really at its driest state at this stage,
it is labelled dried. In this state, it is stored and transported
throughout the world, and commercially marketed as soft,
semi-dry or dry, depending on the date variety.

What further sets this fruit above others is this: besides
enjoying it as a fresh fruit or dessert after meals or between

Ripe red dates, called *berben* in Iraq. In this *khalal* state, they are still firm and moderately sweet.

Clusters of golden ripe dates in the *khalal* stage, when still hard and crunchy, a little astringent and moderately sweet.

meals, in the arid zones, where it grows most successfully, it is the meal itself. The date is an affordable, concentrated energy, staple food, comparable to wheat, potatoes and rice in other parts of the world, where Mother Nature is more generous. It is called 'bread of the desert' and 'cake for the poor'. In its dried form it is an important crop in fighting global hunger. On the high seas in pre-modern times it sustained Arab sailors during their long voyages of trade and discovery. More importantly, with its help they managed to stave off the dangers of scurvy, a deficiency disease to which European sailors were susceptible.

The date tree itself is no less unique – a tall and beautiful palm with evergreen feathery leaves radiating like sun rays

Date groves in Oman, in the southeast corner of the Arabian Peninsula, where date palm cultivation is a mainstay for farmers.

from the top of its single stem. It is both impressively bountiful and versatile. The tree flourishes in arid areas where other trees may barely survive. It is indigenous to the Old World along an area extending from northwest and north Africa, particularly in the Sahara desert oases, through southwestern Asia to India and Pakistan. In Europe today the only place where it is commercially successful is Elche in Spain, whereas in the New World it mostly thrives in the hot and dry region of southern California. In the southern hemisphere its cultivation is increasing at places like the arid regions of Namibia in Africa and Alice Springs in the Northern Territory of Australia.

Its botanical name is *Phoenix dactylifera*, commonly called 'date palm'. To set it apart from its many relatives, which are not as edible, it is sometimes referred to as the 'true date palm' or 'edible date palm'. These relatives include the dwarf date palm (*P. roebelenii*) and Canary Island date palm (*P. canariensis*). These two varieties mostly serve as ornamental trees. The wild Indian date palm (*P. sylvestris*), which is exploited for the sugar derived from its sap, looks very much like the date palm but its fruit is not edible. It is believed to be the ancestor of the true date palm.

What's in a Name?

> They are the most esteemed, affording not only plenty
> of nutriment, but a great abundance of juice; it is from
> these that the principal wines are made in the East.
> These wines are apt to affect the head, a circumstance
> from which the fruit derives its name.
>
> Pliny the Elder (AD 23–79) describing a variety of Middle
> Eastern dates called *caryotae*, 'stupid head'[1]

Phoenix dactylifera is an ancient Greek nomenclature, derived from Phoenicia, the ancient narrow coastal region between the Mediterranean Sea and the Jordan Valley that makes up modern-day Lebanon and parts of Syria, Israel and Palestine. Phoenicia means the 'purple land' in Greek, so called because it was famous for the purple dye extracted from the poisonous sea snail Murex. The date palm used to grow in abundance in that region, and the Greeks thought it was the homeland of the tree. Therefore they gave it the name Phoenix (the tree of Phoenicia) and it became the region's symbol. It figured on Phoenician coins as well as Carthaginian ones, struck in Sicily. To the Roman who could not read

0.9-gram gold tenth-shekel of Carthage (near present-day Tunis), from *c.* 350–320 BC. It features a date palm, which the Greeks called phoenix, 'the tree of Phoenicia'. Carthage was a Phoenician colony.

A traditional Iranian carpet motif, depicting the ancient legend of the fire-bird, or phoenix. It built its nest of cassia twigs and frankincense on top of an old date palm, shown here in a stylized form in the lower left-hand corner.

the Carthaginian language, Punic, the date palm on the coin symbolized Phoenicia, which itself established ancient Carthage, near the present-day site of Tunis.

More romantic, however, are the Greek myths that associate the palm with the fascinating story of the fiery bird that never dies. Writing at the beginning of the first century AD, Pliny the Elder in his *Natural History* tells the legend of the phoenix bird, which lived in the desert of Arabia. It lived to the age of 500, and there was only ever one at a time. It used to build its nest of cassia twigs and frankincense on top of an old date palm. After 500 years, the bird would burn itself in flames ignited by the sun, and a new young phoenix would be reborn from its own ashes. Some say that after 500 years it would lay a single egg and then ignite itself in a pyre of dragon's blood, frankincense and myrrh. The old date palm Pliny mentions in this account is a special variety, called *syagri*, which he further describes:

> We have heard a wonderful story too, relative to this last tree, to the effect that it dies and comes to life again in a similar manner to the phoenix, which, it is generally thought, has borrowed its name from the palm tree, in consequence of this peculiarity; at the moment that I am writing this, that tree is still bearing fruit.[2]

The myth of the phoenix and the date palm is said to have originated in Egypt. Herodotus in the fifth century BC described the phoenix as as a mythical, sacred, female firebird with beautiful gold and red feathers. After it is reborn from the ashes somewhere in Arabia, it carries the ashes of the old phoenix-parent in an egg made of myrrh and deposits it in the Egyptian city Heliopolis ('city of the sun' in Greek).

In the Egyptian mythologies themselves, the phoenix's name is *benu* 'purple heron'. It is mentioned in *The Book of the Dead* and other texts as one of the sacred symbols of worship at Heliopolis and of the sun god Ra. Interestingly, both the date and anything sweet share the name *benu* with this mythical sunbird.

Medieval Arabo-Islamic lore did not connect the legendary phoenix (called *'anqaa* in Arabic) with the date palm. It was Western lore from antiquity onwards that kept the exotic myth of the Arabian tree and the phoenix alive, as displayed in works by Ovid, Dante and Shakespeare. In the poem 'Lover's Martyr (The Phoenix and the Turtle [-dove])', the 'sole Arabian tree' described by Shakespeare is generally believed to be the date palm:

Let the bird of loudest lay
On the sole Arabian tree,
Herald sad and trumpet be:
To whose sound chaste wings obey.

One way of explaining the origins of such fables is the curious growth of the date palm itself. In W. F. Wigston's words,

> It throws its branches every year from the center, and the old ones dying go to form the bark of the tree in a remarkable way, suggesting continual death and rebirth.[3]

Besides, the date seeds are known to possess the ability to stay dormant for many years and germinate when conditions are favourable, which brings to mind an experiment that took place only a few years ago. Two-millennia-old date seeds were discovered near the Dead Sea and were identified as the seeds

Evergreen feathery leaves radiating like sun rays from top of a date-palm trunk.

from the extinct Judean date tree. Several seeds were treated with special growth hormones and within weeks one of them sprouted. The scientists gave it the name Methuselah.[4]

The second part of the name, *dactylifera*, is a combination of *dactylus* 'date' (Greek *dactylos*) and *fero* 'to bear'. Literally, the Greek *dactylus* means 'finger', and the name transferred to the oblong date-fruit itself. In the second century AD this connection had already been established. In Artemidorus' *Book of Dreams*, a man suffering from some ailment in his stomach prayed to the god of healing to cure him. In his dream he saw himself in this god's temple. The god held the fingers of the man's right hand and asked him to eat them. As soon as the man awoke, he ate five dates, and was cured. Artemidorus explains that the dates of the palm tree are called fingers.

Some scholars suggest that *dactylus* is related to the Hebrew and Arabic *deqel / dekel*,[5] which derives from the Semitic root *d-q-l*. The Aramaic *diqla* stands for 'date palm' and 'palm mast', and the Syriac *deql* is a 'date palm'. The similarity is too close to pass as coincidental. I find it intriguing as well that the Tigris (the Greek name for the Mesopotamian river) is called Deqlat in Syriac. In Akkadian, it is Idiqlat/Idiglat (Sumerian 'idekelet'), in Hebrew it is Hiddekel and in Arabic, Dijla. It is highly possible that Tigris originally meant 'the date-palm river'.

European languages adopted the Greek word *dactylifera*, such as the Italian *dattero*, French *datte*, Spanish *datil*, and the English 'date'. In Portuguese, however, the word of choice for the date palm was the Hebrew and Arabic *tamar / tamr*, which originally derived from the Semitic root *t-m-r* (n. *tam[a]r* = palm tree, dates). This is possibly from the Akkadian *damu* (blood), descriptive no doubt of the ripe date, which is usually reddish brown.

Related to *tamr* and *tamar* is the word *tamur*. Medieval Arabic lexicons explain that it designates 'heart' and anything

Folio from *Khamsa* (*Quintet*) by Nizami, showing Layla and her attendants in a date palm grove. Layla is the centrve of the most famous love story in classical Arabic literature. Opaque watercolour, ink and gold on paper, 1548, from Shiraz, Iran.

In Hebrew, the date palm's name, *tamar*, is also a girl's name. A detail from an illustration in Nizami's *Khamsa* (*Quintet*), 1462.

related to it, including of course blood and redness. The word also signifies goodness and anything that stands tall and erect. Both meanings apply to the date palm perfectly.

In Hebrew the name of the tree is also a girl's name. In the Old Testament, King David's son Absalom 'had a fair sister, whose name was Tamar'. Her physical beauty was further emphasized by describing her as a 'woman of fair countenance' (2 Samuel 13:1).

In ancient Greek and Latin, the name *palma* was applied to the edible date palm and its relative the ornamental dwarf palm, which grew in ancient southern Europe. Some scholars argue that *palma* could have been a corruption of *tamar*, which is analogous to the transformation of the biblical Tadmor to the Greco-Latin Palmyra.[6]

The Anatomy of the Date

In his definitive *Natural History of Palms*, E. Corner says of the palm family in general that it is 'the perfect idea, popular or philosophic, of what a plant should be'. It 'stamps itself in grand simplicity on the landscape' of all the warm parts of the earth. He further elaborates:

> All we can say is that the palms are as old, if not older, than any other form of flowering plant and that they have endured while the rest have pressed forward into modern trees, climbers, herbs, and grasses, ramified, extended, twisted, and simplified . . . The palm is an evolutionary challenge, primitive, standardized, and viable.[7]

The average height of a fully mature date palm is about 50 feet (15 metres) and more. It grows slowly, and after 6 to 16

A mature date palm surrounded by its children, the offshoots.

years, numerous suckers sprout around its base. It reaches the zenith of its prime at the age of 100.

Beginning from bottom to top, the palm does not have a taproot like the majority of trees; instead its roots are fibrous. A large number of secondary roots grow out of the bottom of the palm's trunk, and they in turn give off a large number of smaller roots. The secondary roots contain a huge number of air passages. This system enables the palm to withstand and absorb large amounts of water without the risk of rotting, provided the water supply is renewable. The palm likes the water it guzzles to be fresh.

The date palm trunk has no annual growth rings, which reveal other trees' ages. Its main growing point is its head, and the cut-off bases of the leaves as they die protect and strengthen the trunk.

Unlike the stems of most trees, the sole cylindrical stem of the palm does not widen as it grows older once a full crown of leaves – necessary for its survival – has developed. This happens when the stem is well above the ground and is completely covered with the withered leaves, which are usually pruned away. A cross-section of the trunk itself will reveal to the naked eye a close net made up of a huge number of tough fibres that look like strings, which run all along the trunk. These are the tree's vascular bundles, which like arteries conduct the nourishing sap from bottom to top. They are all surrounded by hard tissues, which in turn are surrounded by the bases of the fronds. Thus structured, the trunk is stronger and more resilient than in other trees.

The top of the stem ends with a large terminal bud, from which fresh young leaves develop throughout the growing life of the date palm. This is the palm's heart or 'brain'. Cut it off and the tree dies. Each leaf has a main long tough axis

Young leaves
being protected
by fibrous
sheaths.

Offshoots growing at different levels
on the date palm trunk. The majority
come out at the base of the palm,
where the most moisture is.

called the midrib, with long narrow featherlike leaflets that end with almost needle-like tips, which protect the palm from being swayed or broken by the wind. Along the lower part of the midrib a number of very sharp thorns grow. They help protect the terminal bud from being damaged by large animals. The outer skin of the leaflets is very strong and resistant to the damaging effects of blowing grains of sand. It also protects the underlying cells from dry air. The fronds are un-affected by water, which makes them quite useful for sailors who use them in weaving fishing gadgets. The smaller, younger leaves closer to the centre of the terminal bud are protected by fibrous sheaths, which stretch as the leaves grow larger. These stretched sheaths remain there as a network of tough fibre around the bases of the leaves. While developing, the small leaves are constantly protected from the heat of the sun by their 'big brothers'.

The grown date palm gives birth to offshoots, also called suckers. They evolve from underdeveloped tiny buds, which look like small blisters found in the upper angles between the leaves' stalk bases and the stem of the palm. These buds can appear anywhere along the tree's trunk. In this position, they will always be protected by the bases of the leaves. Most of them do not develop but those that do will become suckers. They stay dormant for many years before they start to grow. Prolonged contact with moist surfaces is what usually triggers them into further growth. That explains why offshoots usu-ally come out at the base of the trunk, close to the moist soil, although they do sometimes develop above soil.

In spring the male and female spathes come out between the bases of the leaves that crown the tree. These are the tough, leathery, long cases that contain the flower clusters, called in-florescence. Green at first, they gradually turn brown, and when fully ripe they dry out and contract under the heat of the sun.

Male flower clusters of a date palm look like small, densely crowded branches.

A date is directly attached to the stalk by means of its calyx.

This causes them to split open, revealing clusters of flowers, each of which has a central stem with 50 to 150-plus branches all radiating from it, looking like a broom. Each branch carries a lot of small, delicate flowers, which the hard spathe protects until they are ready for pollination.

The flowers of the male inflorescence have sacs containing yellowish pollen dust. These pollen sacs normally open up within a couple of hours after the spathe bursts open. The same thing happens to the female spathes when they are ready for fertilization. The female flowers look like oval pearls and are yellowish in hue, but the male ones are like stars, white and waxy. Male flower clusters look like small branches, densely crowded and approximately 6 inches (15 cm) long. The female branches are more than twice as long and less crowded. A slight shake of the male inflorescence will produce a cloud of yellowish dust. On rare occasions a date palm may bear both sexes, in which case it is described as polygamous. When

Stalks of dates, in various stages of ripeness.

neither in bloom nor carrying dates, it is difficult to tell the sex of the tree.

The date is a berry: a simple fruit produced from a single ovary. Its flower has three carpels (female reproductive organs); when pollinated only one develops while the other two abort. The date has a single seed (also known as a stone). If left unpollinated, the growing dates might not have seeds at all, or may develop small deformed ones. In any case, they do not ripen beyond the first stage, when the fruit is hard with a glossy yellow or red skin.

Dates grow in bunches; each bunch has a main stem (axis) from which many stalks branch. The date is directly attached to the stalk by means of its calyx, and when in the moist and soft stage of ripeness, it can easily be pulled off, leaving stone and calyx still attached.

I

Looking after the Date

The offshoot should be planted by a man who possesses
feminine qualities and a moist temperament.
While planting it, he should laugh and be merry
and tell jokes. If he is not in the mood, then he
should at least pretend to be so. This will be good
for the welfare of the growing date palm.

Ibn Wahshiyya, *Nabatean Agriculture* (10th century, Iraq)

The date palm might be a hardy tree but it needs a lot of care
if it is to deliver as expected. The first rule of thumb is to keep
it well watered in a hot, sunny spot. As the Arabs said long
ago, a date palm is at its happiest when its feet are in water and
its head in heaven's fire. The resemblance between date palms
and humans is repeatedly stressed in ancient and medieval
Arab lore. The palm's terminal bud is its head, which encloses
the brain. The tree is said to die suddenly as if of a heart
attack due to stress or an emotional trauma. According to
one of the stories, a date palm groaned when the Prophet
did not preach by its trunk, as his custom was. So he went to
it and embraced it and said to his companions, 'If I had not
embraced it, it would have continued groaning until the day
of resurrection.'[1]

The perfect date palm location with its roots in water and its head 'in heaven's fire': Basra, southern Iraq, 1944.

Like humans, the date palm is said to be sociable. It does well at places bustling with life. The palm may die from sickness or from severe heat. As with women, if the palm gets too fat or too thin, it cannot conceive easily. Like women, the female date palms are impregnated with 'semen' with varying chances of success. They are also similar to women in that both are said to be influenced by the moon. The best time for planting an offshoot is when the moon is full, and while doing so, the planter has to be in a happy mood so that the tree may be blessed by the moon god, who likes merriment.[2] This affinity with the moon is curiously echoed in the language of today's Iraqi Sabians (*Subba* in the Iraqi vernacular), an ancient religious sect. They call the date palm *Sindirka*, 'road to the moon'.

Typical metal work depicting the date palm or *Sindirka*, 'road to the moon', by Iraqi Sabians (*Subba*). This sect is believed to go back to ancient Mesopotamian times.

To reap the benefits of the date palm, the farmer has to be patient. It takes several years for the offshoot to stand on its feet, so to speak, and start producing dates. One of the law codes of the Babylonian king Hammurabi (1728–1686 BC) states:

> When a landlord gave a field to a gardener to set out an orchard, the gardener shall develop the orchard for four years; in the fifth year the owner of the orchard and the gardener shall divide equally.

In the interim, the farmer has to sustain himself with other crops. One way of doing this is to interplant other varieties of trees and herbs. This method is practical for another reason. The higher date palms form a canopy that provides shade

Limestone relief depicting the deportation of captive women from Babylonia, where date palms successfully grew; from the reign of Assyrian King Sennacherib, 705–681 BC.

and protection for other crops. Ancient Sumerian texts mention the coexistence of date palms with other fruit trees, such as pomegranate, apple, peach, fig, apricot, plum, grapevines and citrus; underneath these, seasonal vegetables and herbs were planted. This explains why in the Qur'an date palms are usually mentioned in conjunction with other fruit trees. Date palm orchards today are still exploited in the same manner.

Like builders of skyscrapers, farmers taking care of the palms have to have a good head for heights. During the pollinating and harvesting seasons, they need to climb up the trees to where the action is. The palm climber ties a rope around the rough trunk and his body. Iraqi farmers call this rope *tabliyya*, which even etymologically goes far back in origin to the ancient Mesopotamians, who called it *tabalu*. The

Date palm climber in the oasis region of al-Hasa, in eastern Saudi Arabia.

farmer leans back and literally walks to the top, with the rope being raised at each step to hitch itself on the projections immediately above. This can be seen on a fresco from the palace of Mari dating from the beginning of the second millennium BC. Nowadays we can see the date palm climbers 'walking' up the date palms the same way. I have even seen them climbing not-so-high palms with no support at all.

Date palm climbing is not as easy as it may seem. Falling from a date palm is unfortunately not an uncommon accident among farmers. An ancient Mesopotamian text tells how after his death one farmer who had fallen victim to this accident turned into a demon who appeared intermittently as a

ghost. He is one among many other ghosts who were un-
happy in their lives or died a violent death, which include:

> She who dies a virgin;
> She who dies in childbed;
> He who drowned himself;
> He who had fallen from a palm tree.[3]

In modern groves where the date palm is not indigenous to
the region, as in southern California, three-legged stepladders
are used while the palms are still short. For taller palms farmers use wooden platforms suspended by chains from the top
of the palm, and a ladder is left permanently hanging from
the same place. The farmer carries around a portable ladder
which he uses to get up to the bottom of the hanging one.
Alternatively, tall aluminum ladders are used. They are less
cumbersome and lighter.

Good-quality date palms usually grow from offshoots.
They are the children that grow around the mother, and its
clones, for they share the same genes. They are usually removed when they are three to five years old. The separation
of the offshoot from the mother is a critical job for the
farmer. It is almost like separating a baby from its mother by
severing the umbilical cord – the intertwining complex net of
roots. The offshoots are planted approximately 30 feet (27
metres) apart, with a density of about 50 trees per acre. The
palms begin growing fruits after about five years, and mature
by the tenth year. The palms have to be irrigated profusely,
by means of canals and flooding, but never with rain. Rain is
the palm's enemy because it destroys pollen, stigmas and
ripening dates.

More recently, tissue culture technology has been used
to propagate the date palm. It is an efficient and fast method

Tissue culture, fast and efficient, is the most recent technology used to propagate date palms.

for cloning good-quality date palms. The tissue-cultured palm takes seven years from test tube to first crop. Planting from offshoots can pass on insects and diseases from mother to child; not so with tissue-cultured palms. Very small cuttings are taken from the heart of the palm, which is its growth bud. They are then put in a sterile solution. It takes about a year for the embryos to grow to the point at which they can be cut into pieces. Each piece needs about three months to grow into a seedling. After six more months, these seedlings can be planted. After that, they only need two or three more years to start flowering. In the fourth or fifth year, the palms are mature enough to start producing fruit, which is about three years earlier than traditional propagation by offshoots.

Springtime Chores

In the spring the first task the tree climbers have to perform is to get rid of superfluous offshoots at the base of the tree. Only four to six need to be kept: if all the offshoots are left, they will affect productivity of the crops. The palm usually starts producing offshoots that are good enough to be replanted between the ages of five and twenty. After that, the number diminishes. If the tree is of a desirable quality, more offshoots are allowed to stay.

Next, the dead fronds are pruned, and so are as many as possible of the thorns, which usually grow towards the base of each leaf. These thorns are very strong and might cause serious injury. Nature bestowed them on the date palm as weapons for self-defence. According to popular Muslim tradition, Satan was to blame for these thorns. The story goes that

Offshoots growing around the date palm are its clones, for they share the same genes.

Most of the offshoots are usually separated from their mother when they are three to five years old. If they are all left, they affect the productivity of the tree.

after God created Adam, he asked him to clip his hair and fingernails and bury them. Immediately, a beautiful fully-grown date palm laden with ripe dates sprang from the ground to nourish Adam in the Garden of Eden. At this miracle, Adam fell prostrate in adoration and started worshipping God. Soon enough, Satan appeared and was jealous of the blessings God bestowed upon Adam, and wept so hard that he shed tears of fury. These tears happened to moisten the roots of the date palm and caused thorns to grow at the base of the leaves.

Spring is the time for pollination, which has to be done manually. From early times, the Mesopotamian farmers knew about the dioecious nature of the date palm. They called the

Strong thorns protecting inflorescence sheaths. They are the palm's weapon for self-defence.

male palm *gishimmaru zakiru*, and the female *gishimmaru zin-nishtu*. They also practiced the act of pollination themselves to ensure fertility. Law item 64 in the codes of the Babylonian King Hammurabi states:

> If a landlord gave his orchard to a gardener to pollinate, the gardener shall give to the owner of the orchard two-thirds of the produce of the orchard as rent of the orchard as long as the orchard is held, with himself taking one-third.

The artistic depiction of the tree of life in Assyrian art, showing a stylized date palm with a genius holding a bucket in one hand and a cone-like object in the other, has been interpreted by some Assyriologists as a pollinating act. In ancient times, the month during which the palms were fertilized bore the name of the Date Month. At this time, they celebrated the marriage festival of all the gods and goddesses. In his visit to Babylon in the fifth century BC, Herodotus noticed that the Babylonians 'tie the fruit of the male-palms . . . to the branches of the date-bearing palm, to let the gall-fly enter the dates and ripen them, and to prevent the fruit from falling off'.[4] Pliny had a better idea of how it was done:

> So well, indeed, is this sexual union between them under-
> stood, that it has been imagined even that fecundation
> may be ensured through the agency of man, by means of

Harvested male pollen. To its right is the shaker farmers use to dust the female date flowers with pollen, in addition to the male flower twigs inserted amongst the female flowers.

the blossoms and the down gathered from off the male
trees, and, indeed, sometimes by only sprinkling the dust
from off them on the female trees.[5]

First, the male pollen has to be harvested and then applied
to the opened-up female inflorescence. This requires several
journeys up and down the palm. On average, pollen from one
male palm will be enough to fertilize about 50 females. Any
excess male pollen can be stored for the following year. Growing in nature, there would be more males around, enough to
pollinate the females by wind, but in commercial orchards
space and labour are too precious to waste on useless males.

Timing is critical for successful pollination. The female
flowers will no longer be receptive to the pollen after a few
days of opening up. A light dusting of pollen and twigs inserted among the female strands will do the job. In some
modern groves, the pollen is inducted by means of large air
blowers, which makes the labour-intensive manual method
unnecessary, but this is costly.

Summer Chores

With some date varieties, such as *medjool*, as the clusters start
growing the date strands are thinned. Almost half of them are
removed to ensure a harvest of impressively large dates, as
this will allow more nourishment for the remaining fruits. To
get to the edible phase, the dates first grow into *chimri*. At this
unripe stage they are green and sour. As the clusters grow
larger and heavier, they tend to bend the stalk. The farmers
might tie the clusters or adjust them so that they are supported by the bases of the fronds. This makes the crown of
the date palm look as if it were wearing a heavy necklace.

An Egyptian farmer working in a date palm grove in the Siwa oasis in Egypt at the edge of the Great Sand Sea near the eastern Libyan border, famous for its dates and olives.

On average, good date palm varieties may yield around 100 lb (45 kg) of fruit, and sometimes even more.

While growing the sweet dates have to be protected from several enemies, such as wasps and birds. Farmers usually use mats woven of palm fronds or paper bags to loosely cover the clusters. As a decoy, they leave a few uncovered ones to attract the birds away from the rest. In Baghdad the enemy is the jerboa (*jredi 'l-nakhal*), a rat-like rodent, and in other, drier regions, locusts play havoc with all crops. In Pakistan and India date palms have to be protected from parrots and monkeys. A watchman is usually appointed to keep them away by shouting or throwing stones at them. He also hangs bells and other noise-making devices and shakes them periodically. And, of course, there are the human enemies, thieves who go to the orchards under the cover of the dark night, some of

Clusters heavily laden with ripening dates, which farmers let rest on the fronds to prevent their stalks from breaking.

Clusters of dates in the *chimri* unripe stage, green and sour.

them naked; when surprised by a watchdog, they stand on all fours and scare it away.

Date palms are susceptible to pests and diseases such as bayoud, for which some sort of fungus is to blame. This disease causes a major decline in production where it is present, and is a particular problem in Morocco and western Algeria. The most troublesome pest is the scale insect, and in Baghdad the enemy is the palm borer, *chirneeb*. In modern times, fumigation is used to fight them. Before that, the farmers in their helplessness resorted to superstition. It was common to protect date palm groves by hanging a sheep skull with horns on a post. The horns were believed to have some magical protective powers against evil; this no doubt had its roots in ancient practices.

Nature itself can sometimes be an enemy, even in the most favourable zones. Unusual extreme drought may occur

Unexpected snow storm in Palm Springs in the desert area of southern California, around the beginning of the 20th century. Growing date palms has proved quite successful in this dry and hot region, but a sudden drop in temperature or a snow storm usually ruins the growing dates.

Fully ripe dates in the *rutab* stage, sweet and soft.

in the oases districts. Sandstorms can spoil the dates as the sand speckles stick to the maturing fruits. Unseasonal humidity or cool weather, which can occur in Tunisia, Algeria and California, or rain in areas exposed to the monsoon, as in Punjab, will definitely harm the fruit as it will not ripen properly or will rot and go to waste.

When harvest time comes the climbers have to perform several trips to the top. This is partly because the dates do not ripen all at the same time, and also because the dates are edible in three stages of ripeness, *khalal* (still hard and crunchy), *rutab* (soft) and *tamr* (dried). With some varieties it is possible to

A processing facility in Saudi Arabia where naturally dried dates, *tamr*, are sorted, graded and packaged.

cut off the entire cluster and use the dates, but some dates, such as *medjool*, are too expensive to be treated casually. Instead, they are picked gradually as they ripen. In many places dates are still picked by hand, but in modern groves in California and Saudi Arabia machines are used to shake the palm and cause the dates to fall.

In perfect growing conditions the dates reach the *tamr* stage quite nicely and they dry up naturally on the tree in the sun. However, in areas where rain is a possibility at the end of the maturation season, as in California, as soon as dates reach *tamr* stage they are harvested and spread in ventilated places to dry artificially.

When properly dried, naturally or artificially, dates are ready to store. For marketing purposes, they are taken to the processing facilities where they are washed, air-dried, sorted, graded and packaged. While performing these tasks, the dates

A package of *ma'moul* pastries, filled with excellent Saudi dates, as the label boasts.

have to be handled with extreme care because they are relatively soft, and to bring a good market price they have to keep their shape. However, with very soft and sticky date varieties this is not as critical since they will be pressed into date paste anyway. Dates of low quality are usually packaged and transported in bulk in large containers such as boxes, baskets made of woven date palm fronds, or skins. Fancy dates are more carefully handled. As early as the 1920s, mechanisms to fumigate and pasteurize the dates and steam them to add gloss and improve their appearance were introduced to Basra, the centre for growing dates in Iraq at the time. Before Algeria and Tunisia started packaging their own *deglet noor* dates, the dates used to be exported to Marseilles, where they were packaged and re-exported to Europe.

In their dry preserved form, excellent date varieties, called dessert dates, are carefully and attractively packaged whole and complete with seeds, unless they are filled with nuts. The American name for the date seed is 'pit', whereas in the UK it is 'stone', and dates sold with seeds removed are labelled 'stoned'. An anecdote goes that it occurred to one of the British packers to improve on this name,

> perhaps by analogy with words like decorticated [peeled], and [he] advertised his dates as 'Destoned'. This led a perplexed member of the House of Commons to ask during a debate on proposed alterations in customs duties whether the destined date was a stoned one that had its stone put back again.[6]

Cooking dates are usually stoned. However, no dependable methods have yet been found to ensure that all seeds are removed, which explains the warnings we read on date packages today. It seems that up until recently in the US, manufacturers were obligated by law to compensate customers for any damages incurred by unexpected seeds: 'If a package from which the customer took the date is labeled "pitted," he may claim from the packers, generally successfully, 50 or even 100 dollars in compensation.'[7]

Some date varieties do not make it to the dried *tamr* stage because they have too much natural moisture. The Iraqi ruby-red *berben*, for instance, and the Punjabi *ghatti*, large and purple, are harvested in the *khalal* and *rutab* stages and are eaten within a few days as fresh fruit; after that they start to ferment. But they certainly can last longer at places where refrigeration

Date auction at a market-place in Oman.

and freezing amenities are available. Dates might also be eaten
fresh or kept refrigerated in marginal areas where it is hot
enough but too humid for dates to dry, as on the Libyan and
Arab Gulf coasts.

At places where growing conditions are not perfect, there
are many ways to salvage the fruit. Extremely dry weather, for
instance, will cause dates to shrivel on the palm, as in Sudan.
Therefore the dates are picked when just mature and then
ripened in jars to prevent loss of moisture. In Punjab, where
the monsoon comes before dates can fully ripen, they are harvested and preserved in jars, but this time to protect them
from excessive moisture.

Sometimes *khalal* dates are artificially ripened to *rutab*
state for a variety of reasons. It could be that the dates will be
damaged by insects or rain if they are left on trees, or that they
will not ripen naturally due to low temperatures. In Egypt, the
south coast of Arabia and Mexico the dates are spread on

mats in one layer and exposed to the sun for a week or so. In Lower Egypt they are steeped in brine to hasten ripening. Dates might be sprinkled with vinegar and kept in closed barrels for a day, but the flavour will not be so good. Bruising *khalal* is another method. In Pakistan, for instance, *khalal* dates are beaten with a stick to let the astringent tannin escape with the running juice, and then wrapped in blankets and left overnight. People do this for no better reason than poverty and hunger, for they cannot afford to wait for the dates to ripen fully. In Australia entire clusters are kept covered with the cut end of the cluster in water until the dates are fully ripe. Sometimes *khalal* are further matured and sweetened by keeping them in date syrup or honey. Freezing *khalal* will work the same way.

The parthenocarpic (literally 'virgin') seedless dates that grow from unfertilized female inflorescence are of low quality. They are small with thin flesh, and are not as sweet or flavourful as the pollinated ones because they never fully mature. People in the Middle East find them useful for pickling, and some growers at places like southern California ripen them by treating them with heated air saturated with moisture.

Khalal dates may be dried without passing through the *rutab* stage. This is usually done with varieties of inferior quality that do not ripen well, or that grow in places where temperatures are not high enough, or sometimes it is simply done due to a surplus that will ferment and rot otherwise. Dates preserved this way are called *khalal matboukh* (cooked), and are prepared by boiling fresh *khalal* dates in a large pot for 20 to 40 minutes. They are then drained and spread on mats and dried in the sun. They will be hard but brittle and taste sweet. They are very popular in Iraq and other Gulf countries and Punjab, where they are called *bhugrian*, but unknown in North Africa.

Sexual Excursions:
The Secret Life of the Date Palm

In a forest of natural growth . . . many female
trees may be seen surrounding a single male with
downcast heads and a foliage that seems to
be bowing caressingly towards it.
Pliny the Elder, *Natural History*[8]

Imagine a world where humans are prohibited from breeding through sex and propagation is conducted purely by the indifferent means of cloning chosen races, who have been proven by experience to possess good qualities. This was what man did to the date palms thousands of years ago, in the name of 'cultivation'.

Date palms in their natural state lived like human beings. Males and females of almost equal numbers grew together, and mated sexually. Though some chose to confine themselves to a preferred mate, date palms overall were notoriously promiscuous, and the bastardly offspring *deqel* was the norm. The mating game among the palms for thousands upon thousands of years played havoc with their genes. Like humans, each date palm has its own unique chain of DNA.

When man tasted the date, he coveted it and soon realized that the way the date palms were naturally propagating would not provide dates that were sufficiently satisfactory, either in quantity or quality. The first thing he did was to dispense with most of the male palms, since only the females grow fruit. If one male is enough to impregnate 50 females, why waste space, time and hard work on them? Therefore, the male role was relegated by man to that of a 'sperm donor'; the fun was over.

Folio from *'Aja'ib al-Makhluqat* (God's Amazing Creations) by al-Qazwini, which reveals the secret lives of dates palms. Early 15th century, opaque watercolour, ink and gold on paper. Iraq or Eastern Turkey.

In any given orchard, ideally only a few male palms were allowed, preferably vigorous, virile ones, which produce plenty of good and healthy male inflorescence. They were kept in a separate corner to prevent them from illicit meddling with the females. The female palms in a sense became man's harem, and were impregnated by him manually through the method of dusting them with the male pollen and inserting sprigs of the male inflorescence among their strands to ensure fertilization. And this marriage of the palms has been performed every spring ever since.

The pollinated palms will in due time grow dates and these dates have seeds, which nature intended for the propagation of the species. But seeds are not good enough, as the new generation will not be exactly similar to the mother, as with humans. Besides, there is a 50/50 chance that the seedlings will turn out to be males. Therefore man resorted to vegetative propagation, which is a sort of cloning. It surely is less romantic but gives perfect results every time it is used; no chance is allowed!

The babies growing around the palm can be successfully separated and planted. The child extends its own net of roots and grows into a productive female, which carries its mother's genes. When mature enough and fertilized with whatever pollen is available, regardless of male quality, it will still produce the same variety of date. The male genes are irrelevant here because the edible part of fruit formed as the immediate result of pollination is not affected by the character of the male used, which also explains the lack of incentive to breed good male trees on regular basis, and hence the scarcity of good males. Therefore, as soon as a desirable variety of tree is discovered, the only option to breed is through its offshoots, to stop it from metamorphosing any more.

This is the life male and female date palms have led ever since domestication. However, incidents of rebelliousness do exist. One of the stories in al-Qazwini's fifteenth-century *'Aja'ib al-Makhluqat* (God's amazing creations) tells the story of a farmer from Arabia who had a female palm that usually bore abundantly, but had stopped producing for two consecutive years. They called in a connoisseur in the affairs of the palms. After climbing up and inspecting it, he came down announcing there was nothing wrong physically with the palm. Then he looked left and looked right, and finally espied a male palm at a short distance. His verdict was that the tree was in love with that date palm. 'Pollinate it from him only', he advised. Sure enough, the story goes, after the farmer did so, the tree resumed its old ways.

2

Date Varieties

Indeed when in a fresh state, [dates] are so remarkably luscious,
that there would be no end to eating them, were it not for fear
of the dangerous consequences that would be sure to ensue.
Pliny the Elder

Of date-growing palms encountered in foreign lands, Pliny
the Elder says, 'we find nine and forty different kinds of
palm trees, if any one will be at the trouble of enumerating
all their various barbarous names'. I am afraid that even today
when discussing the date fruit, we have no other choice but
use its 'barbarous' names, which happen to be Arabic more
often than not, for nowhere has the date palm been as central to people's economic and cultural lives as it has been in
the Middle East. Over long centuries of cultivating the palm,
they developed a rich date-related repertoire of technical vo-
cabulary for which there is no equivalent in other languages.
As early as ancient Mesopotamia, the language of dates was
advanced and highly specialized, and by the medieval era the
Arabs' knowledge of the field had reached its highest level.
Arabic names of dates were already in circulation in classical
antiquity, judging from Pliny's mention of a sticky and sweet
date that grew in Arabia, which he calls *dablan* (soft).

Ripening red dates in the *khalal* stage, sweet but still crunchy.

Pliny describes several date varieties in some detail, such as the royal dates in the inaccessible gardens near Babylonia and the whitish round *margarides*, which resemble pearls. The *syagrus* are 'large, hard, and of a rough appearance, and differing in taste from all other kinds, having a sort of wild flavor peculiar to itself, and not unlike that of the flesh of the wild boar'. The *caryotae* or 'stupid head' are used in making wine, and the *patetae* are so juicy that they crack open even while still on the tree. Some say the name derives from Syriac or Hebrew *patach*, meaning 'open up'. Pliny also mentions dates of a drier nature growing especially in Ethiopia, where some kinds are so dry and brittle that they can be ground into flour and kneaded into bread. As for dates in Thebes, they are preserved in jars while still fresh. He adds they need to be heated in the oven before eating. Apparently, they did not ripen well naturally.

The majority of dates, Pliny says, are the ordinary *trage-mata*. Their name is *balani*, and they come in various shapes and colours: round, oblong, dark, red or whitish.[1] *Balanitis* in Greek is 'acorn', and it seems that calling dates 'acorn' has Semitic roots. In Syriac, for instance, the generic name for the date is *balloota saqla*, 'smooth acorn'.[2]

As fond as the Greeks and Romans were of the date, they had to be content mostly with the ordinary *tragemata*, the imported varieties of *balani*, mostly from Egypt and Phoenicia, and these were not cheap. Only the affluent households had access to them. In the fourth century BC Xenophon described dates he encountered on his Persian expedition:

> As to the palm dates themselves, it was noticeable that the sort which we are accustomed to see in Greece were set aside for the domestic servants; those put aside for the masters are choice fruit, and are simply marvellous for their beauty and size, looking like great golden lumps of amber; some specimens they dried and preserved as sweetmeats. Sweet enough they were as an accompaniment of wine, but apt to give headache.[3]

In the long history of the tree's cultivation, several thousands of varieties have been established. This happens because the date palm is dioecious: that is, the male and female are separate. When it was domesticated, the evolution of unpredictable varieties was somewhat checked by planting the offshoots of the mother. Still, unpredictable new varieties do come out from seedlings of unknown parentage. Such bastardly new breeds are called *deqel* in Arabic, and described as *mejhool* (unknown). Often, they turn out to be disappointing unproductive males or females with inferior qualities. Therefore the number of varieties is not the criterion for judging the qualitative productivity of a region. The Punjab region, for instance, grows 300 varieties, of which only a handful are good, because they were all originally propagated from seeds. In Iraq, the number of good-quality varieties is considerably higher, due to the long experience and skill acquired over the centuries of cultivating the palm and manipulating its genes.

If the new *deqel* turns out to produce a desirable variety – which is quite unusual but does happen – farmers start propagating it from its offshoots to stop further changes in its genes. This new breed will be given a name, perhaps after the person who planted it if known, the place where it was found, or a special physical feature.

Dried date varieties grown in different regions of Saudi Arabia. *'Ajwa* on the right top corner is the date of Medina, in the western region, said to be the Prophet's favorite date. On the lower right corner is *khalasa/khlas*, the ultimate date of Saudi Arabia.

A famous date variety which started as *deqel* is the North African light-golden *deglet noor*, 'date of light', so called because it is almost translucent; you may even see the seed when the date is held up to the sun. Its native region is the Algerian and Tunisian oases in the Sahara. It was first discovered in the seventeenth century and was immediately recognized as an excellent variety. Legend has it that the date was called after a pious woman called Lalla Noora, who used to live in the oases district. She was too poor to buy a rosary to repeat the 99 names of God, so she made one with 99 date seeds. When she died the people who discovered her body buried her on the spot. The 99 seeds took roots and grew into palms that carried wonderful dates, which people called *deglet Noora*.[4] According to another version, the seeds were from the date palm in the courtyard of the house of the Prophet's wife 'Aisha in Medina, the 'City of Light'.

Another famous *deqel* date of unknown parentage is the large, sweet and succulent *medjool*. It is so called because originally it was a *mejhool* date (of unknown lineage). In fact, *mejhool* was the name by which it was known in commerce in the Tafilatet region in Morocco and Southern Algeria. As to when it was discovered, this is still unknown. No foreign travellers to the Tafilatet oases in the nineteenth century mentioned a date of this name. However, quite possibly it might have passed by another name, *medqool* (from *deqel*),[5] which is indeed synonymous with *mejhool*.

The Tafilatet oasis, where the *mejhool* date was discovered, is in the Moroccan interior. The region has been famous for its dates for many centuries, due to its extended summer heat, an abundant water supply and skilful farmers, who were originally immigrants from Filal, a district in Arabia.[6] Up until the beginning of the twentieth century, *mejhool* was a rare variety. It was grown for export only and its offshoots were kept under lock and key. The villagers who grew them lived on inferior dates.

While *medjool* and *deglet noor* dates are known worldwide, there are other varieties of comparable excellence known only in their native regions and surrounding areas. More than 600 excellent date varieties grow in the Middle East.[7] Each region with a long tradition in growing dates has its own distinct varieties, which are usually given names reflective of a place or a person's name, or they might be descriptive of the date's appearance, taste, texture and so on. Some varieties are given curious names like *beidh il-bilbil* (nightingale's eggs), *asabi' il-'aroos* (bride's fingers), *mlabbas il-'ajooz* (old woman's candy) and *khasawi il-baghal* (mule's testicles).

Iraq has the lion's share of the good varieties. *Zahdi* (*zahidi*, *azadi*) is the main commercial date in Baghdad. It is cheap, resilient and keeps well in any ripening state. Due to its high sugar content, it is used in making the famous Iraqi distilled alcoholic beverage *arak*. *Khistawi*, another Baghdad speciality, is a delicious dessert date. *Hillawi*, named after the city of Hilla south of Baghdad, is more commonly identified as *halawi* (the sweet one) outside Iraq. It ripens early, bears heavily, packs well and keeps well. *Khadhrawi* is the exquisite sweet green date. *Ista'amran* (corruption of *Usta 'Umran*) is a widely consumed date, also called *sayir*. *Barhi* is deemed the best date in Basra. Its name derives from *barih*, 'hot wind', which blows from the Gulf during the summer. The most popular dry date is *ashrasi*, which is eaten with walnuts or pounded with sesame paste into a sweetmeat called *madgooga*.

In Egypt the valued date is *hayani*, named after the village of Hayan, also called *birkawi* and *birkat al-hajj*, 'pilgrim's pond', after an oasis near Cairo where annual caravans to Mecca used to make their first stop in pre-modern times. It is a versatile date which can be sold practically all year round

Assortment of dried dates purchased from Coachella Valley in Southern California. The largest and most popular is *medjool* (right-side row).

if frozen immediately after harvest. *Saidi* (*sa'idi*) dates, from the southern region Sa'id, are a dry variety somewhat similar to the Iraqi *ashrasi*, but not as hard. In the month of Ramadan, when consumption of dates reaches its highest level because of fasting by Muslims, Egyptian fruit vendors follow an amusing rating system to lure buyers. They nickname excellent varieties after celebrities, be they politicians, football players or movie stars. During Ramadan of 2009, the 'Obama' date was the most expensive.

In Tunisia, *manakhir* (nose-like) is large, soft and dark, and somewhat similar to *deglet noor* in flavour. It is a rare date. A distinguished date in Algeria is *thoori* (*tsuri*), a naturally dry date also known as 'bread date'; it is sweet but hard and brittle. In southern Iran, a fine sweet variety grows, characterized by its blackish colour, which might be the reason why it is called *mazafati* (from *zift* 'pitch'). *'Ajwa* is another dark and sweet date. It is the date of Medina in West Arabia, and the Prophet's favourite date. In Oman, Gulf countries and inland Arabia, an interesting soft date called *bu narinja* (orange colour) is a favourite variety similar in appearance to *khalasa* (quintessence), which is the ultimate date of Saudi Arabia. The *khalasa* date has a complex taste which can only be appreciated by keeping the date in your mouth and letting it slowly release its magic of 'flavors of honey, sweet potatoes, sugarcane, and caramel', soon to be joined by 'a more subtle, slightly nutty flavor infused with a rich note of taffy'.[8]

Most of these dates were introduced to southern California at the beginning of the twentieth century.

3
The 360 Uses of the Date Palm

The gardener speaks well of me; of use to both slave and official.
My fruit makes the infant grow. Grown men also eat my fruit.
Debate between the Tamarisk and the Date Palm
(Akkadian text, *c.* 1300 BC).

The date palm has never been short of people to sing its
praises. It is principally a food tree of course, but man has
certainly found ways of using every other part of it. The
subject of an ancient Akkadian fable is a debate between the
tamarisk and the date palm, which emphasizes the value of
the latter to people at the time. It tells how the king planted
a date palm in his palace and filled the area around it with
tamarisk. In the shade of the tamarisk, meals were set out,
but in the shade of the date palm songs were composed,
drums were played, people were merry and the palace rejoiced.
In this debate, the date palm boasts that it is the master of
every craft: all the farmers' equipment – rein, whip, rope,
seeder-plow, harness and so on – is made from it. The palm
further boasts:

> The orphan girl, the widow, the poor man
> Eat without stint my sweet dates.[1]

A road lined with date palms in Basra in southern Iraq, 1944.

Echoing this 'song of the palm', Strabo (*c.* 64 BC–AD 24), in his account on Babylon, mentions that the date palm furnished its people with bread, wine, vinegar and meal. All kinds of woven articles are also made from it. The seeds are used in braziers instead of charcoal, and when softened by being soaked in water, they become food for fattening oxen and sheep. Strabo also mentions a Persian hymn, Plutarch says Babylonian, which sums up the 360 useful properties of the date palm.[2] This was the ancients' way of saying that the date palm was to them the perfect tree.

Following is an attempt to describe the ways and means in which the date palm and its fruit have been serving humanity. My list, alas, is no match for the ancients' 360 uses.

A group of men feasting under the cooling shade of date palms in al-Jawf province in northern Saudi Arabia, bordering Jordan.

Useful Inedibles

As well as in groves, date palms were traditionally planted next to houses. Not only did they provide much-needed cooling shade, but they also worked as air filters. The fronds close to the upper openings of air circulation passages would cleanse the air of dust before it got into the house.

The trunks were made into light bridges, wharfs and rafts. They were cut in half, and with the inside cored out, they worked as open pipes (aqueducts) to irrigate lands. Builders used them for doors, roofs, steps and fences. Tradition has it that the Prophet's first mosque in Medina, built around AD 630, was constructed almost entirely of palm trunks, and the thatching and prayer mats of the leaves. A common sight in rural areas in Iraq during religious feasts are makeshift amusement parks for children with swings and Ferris wheels

A large house surrounded by date palms in an oasis in Oman.

Ornamental date palms in Indian Wells in Coachella Valley, California. The trees are planted in rows after the traditional way of the Old World.

constructed from the trunks. It needs to be mentioned, though, that the trunks of female palms were rarely cut down for building and other purposes. Only old trees or males were used. In olden times, date palm trunks also functioned as a very cruel instrument for capital punishment: criminals were fastened to them until they died. In the Qur'anic verses on Moses 20:71, for instance, the Pharaoh threatened his magicians, who believed in the message of Moses, saying he would affix them (Arabic verb *salaba*) to date palm trunks after cutting off their hands and feet.

The fronds have always been used as decorations for national and religious festivals. For more earthly purposes, they make sheltering roofs, mats, screens and baskets. Brooms are made by trimming the leaflets and binding them together. The entire frond is used to dust walls and ceilings and get rid of cobwebs. Small hand-held fans are woven from the leaflets, and are very refreshing when sprinkled with water in the summer. In the past, bundles of leaves were used as dams by reinforcing them with mud.

When the leaf is stripped of its leaflets, the remaining midrib makes light furniture, crates and cages. The bases of the fronds, large and wide, are used for fuel, and until recently as floats for teaching children to swim in the river Tigris. They also functioned as writing material: in the early days of Islam in the sixth century AD Muslim scribes preserved verses of the Qur'an on them.

The fibre from the old leaf sheaths, which surrounds the bases of the leaves, is good for ropes and rugs, cables and riggings for boats, and nets for sailors. Because of its neutral taste it is used to top vegetables pickled in jars to keep them submerged in liquid, and stuffed into large Arabian coffee pots to strain the coffee while pouring it. The long thorns are used as needles and picks.

Modern technology has found more means of exploiting the tree. The processed leaflets combined with ground-up peanut shells and corncobs are used for making insulating boards, and the leaf bases have been found to be a good source of cellulose pulp, which is used in making walking sticks, brooms, fishing floats and fuel.

Edibles

Of the edible parts of the tree, the terminal bud or heart (Arabic *jummar*) is a delicacy known from ancient times. It was described as having 'a peculiarly pleasant taste', but being apt to cause headaches. It was valued for its aphrodisiac properties and was included in wedding gifts. It is still considered a delicacy, and is usually eaten raw as a snack food. Since removing the heart kills the palm, this is normally done with trees past their prime.

When the heart is cut out for eating, the cavity gradually fills with a thick, sweet fluid, which is the tree's sap. It is consumed as a refreshing drink, but in a few hours it ferments and turns into a highly intoxicating wine. In olden times, it was made even stronger by enhancing it with *harmal* (seeds of rue). Again, this is normally done only to trees past their prime, or in cases where the water source for them is gone, as when wells dry up in oases. Three or four quarts (4 litres) of sap may be obtained daily from a single palm. After a couple of weeks, the quantity decreases and after a couple of months or so, the trunk becomes dry and the tree dies. Sap may also be extracted by tapping a healthy palm with its head still on. This is performed by carefully making V-shaped incisions in the crown, and attaching vessels to them to receive the sap. But this is not to be done more than two or three times in the life of a healthy palm, as tapping reduces date production drastically and causes the tree's death if repeated excessively. Tapping for sugar or wine is usually done with the wild date palm, *Phoenix sylvestris*, which grows abundantly in India. The ancient Egyptians had a peculiar use for palm wine: it cleansed the cavities of mummified corpses, according to Herodotus.

The dates themselves are sought-after even when they are still inflorescence in spathes, both male and female. They are eaten raw or boiled, and an aromatic liquid is extracted by distillation from the fresh spathes themselves. Indeed, they have always been regarded as a highly aphrodisiac food. The name for the male inflorescence in Arabic is '*Ateel*, which in medieval times was also a common man's name, implying masculine virility. Incidentally, this brings to mind the Shakespearean Moorish general Othello, for whose name no convincing etymology has yet been found. In the play's primary source, the Italian story of *Un Capitano Moro*, no name is given to the character. However, we know that around 1600 several Moorish delegations came to England, and it is not far-fetched to conjecture that Shakespeare might have picked up the name 'Ateel for his Moorish hero, but not before giving it an Italian ring.

And as soon as the dates ripen, what's not to do with them? In ancient Mesopotamia, royal fruitcakes (Sumerian *goog*, from which *ka'k* and cake probably derived) were made with dates along with raisins and figs, and the pastrycooks of the ancient Egyptian 'cake-room' were called 'workers in dates'.[3] In the kitchen pantries of classical antiquity, the date was an indispensable ingredient, according to Apicius' list. A delicious 'honey' called *dibs*, extracted from the sweet, syrupy, dried dates, was known from ancient times. It was an important date product, used for sweetening puddings, fruitcakes and sweetmeats.

Delicious dip of date syrup and ground sesame *tahini* (*dibs w-rashi*), a popular Iraqi snack (see pp. 112–13 for details).

Nowadays, the date is processed into many new products, such as sparkling drinks from date juice, used in some Islamic countries as a non-alcoholic version of champagne. Date sugar or date crystals are made by grinding hard dates. Other products include date jam, date pickles and date-butter spread. For non-human consumption, dates are dehydrated, ground and mixed with grain for a nutritious stock feed. Dried dates are fed to camels, horses and dogs in the Sahara.

From ripe dates or date syrup, a reddish variety of vinegar is made, as well as wine. Both were made from ancient times. In his *Natural History* Pliny says that date wine was quite common in all the countries of the East, and describes how it was made. Ripe dates are steeped in water for some time and then strained.[4] It is to be assumed that the resulting liquid was left in jars to ferment. The Arabs of the pre-Islamic era, and even afterwards, were quite fond of date wine. Generally, observant Muslims used to drink it within three days; after that it was not permissible. From references to wine during the early Islamic period, we learn that date wine was made by mixing ripe dates (*tamr*) with fresh and still crunchy dates (*busr/khalal*), which provided the astringent tannin that ripe dates lack. In modern Iraq date wine is no longer used. Instead, dates are left to ferment in water and then distilled into a potent water-like liquid flavoured with mastic gum. It is called *araq* (literally 'sweating') and served diluted with water, which changes it into a milk-like liquid. In its effect, it has been compared to absinthe.

We eat the dates and mindlessly throw the seeds away. In rural areas seeds are useful. Fake coffee is made by roasting and grinding them. Finely ground seeds are mixed with flour to make bread in times of scarcity. They are soaked in water until soft and then fed to the farm animals. Dried and ground up, they are included in chicken feed. The seeds also make good charcoal. In the past, they were strung in necklaces and used as counters in games children played.

Dates are Good for You

And shake the trunk of the palm tree towards thee.
It will drop fresh ripe dates upon thee.
So eat and drink, and let thine eyes be gladdened!
Qur'anic verses on Mary in labour[5]

Islamic Arab lore gives particular attention to the date and its benefits. If we believe all that was said about it, it was indeed to them the miracle food. The Prophet himself endorsed the date by saying that having seven dates a day will be one's safeguard against poison and witchcraft all day long. His food was mostly dates along with a drink of milk/yoghurt or just water. He also loved to eat dates with cucumber. His favourite

Date chutney cooking on stove (see recipe, pp. 117–18).

date was the *'ajwa* of his city al-Medina, which he described as the food of heaven. Its name derives from the Arabic verb *'aja*, which comes from weaning children by giving them food other than milk. Weaned children used to be given this date for nutrition and to chew on. This triad of mother-child-date has been an important motif in Islamic lore. It was supported by the Qur'anic verses on Mary and birth of Jesus. But the idea of the benefits of dates for the mother both in labour and while breastfeeding has been around since much earlier than Islam itself.

In Pseudo Matthew, Mary, Joseph and Jesus stop by a date palm during their flight to Egypt after the Nativity. Mary asks for fruit and the tree bends its branches so that she may pick the dates. This was one of several circulated gospels from the times of the early Church. Much earlier than this, a 700 BC basalt relief was excavated in the ancient site of Cilicia (Asia Minor) in southeastern Turkey, which at the time was part of the Assyrian empire. It depicts a mother suckling her baby next to a date palm laden with date clusters, a scene touchingly reminiscent of Mary and the Child. In Greek myths Leto, wife of Zeus, clasped a palm-tree and an olive-tree when she was about to give birth to the divine twins Apollo and Artemis.

Achille Martinet after a painting by Raphael, Virgin and Child seated at the bottom of a palm tree, and behind them two young figures picking dates from the tree, 1845, etching and engraving on chine collé.

Assyrian upright stone-block showing mother nursing a child, with a date palm in the background. Karatepe, southern Turkey, c. 700 BC.

This bond between women in labour and the date palm has its earliest roots in the Sumerian legends revolving around Inanna (Akkadian Ishtar), the goddess of love and procreation, which naturally include motherhood and childbirth. The date palm was her symbol and abode. Inanna describes herself thus:

> Maiden of the place of begetting am I;
> In the Home where the mother gives birth, a protecting shadow am I.[6]

One of the Hebrew versions of the name of Ishtar was Tamar, and *tamar* is Hebrew for palm and date. In another

Sumerian poem, there is a prayer invoking Inanna uttered by a humble woman, who is in the throes of an apparently out-of-wedlock childbirth:

> In the day of the birth of my infant, my eyes were troubled.
> My hands are stretched out, to the queen of Heaven I pray.
> Begetting mother thou art, spare me in my shame.[7]

This is reminiscent of the description of Mary in labour in the Qur'an. When 'the throes of childbirth compelled her to betake herself to the trunk of a palm tree. She said: Oh, would that I had died before this, and had been a thing quite forgotten.'[8]

Medicinal use of the palm and its dates is well documented in Assyrian cuneiform tablets. From Assyrian herbal texts, we learn that it was used to cure coughs, earache and stomach-ache. It was made into poultices to cure blisters and bruises, fought demons and so on.[9] In Sumerian mythology the date palm was symbolically described as a healing house. In ancient Egypt the date and its juice had more or less similar uses. For children's coughs, for instance, dried dates were crushed and mixed with their milk.

A not-well-kept secret in Islamic folk medicine is the aphrodisiac potency of the date, date palm heart (terminal crown) and date inflorescence. Grooms are advised to eat one pound (half a kilo) of dates on the day of their wedding to ensure the wedding night goes smoothly. Dates are some-times combined with other foods to enhance their aphrodisiac properties.

Modern medicine seems to support many of the claims heaped on dates and give a nod of approval to the custom of Muslims breaking their long fast during the month of Ramadan with a few dates and some milk or yoghurt, following the tradition of the Prophet. While the dates provide the body with the needed nourishment fast, milk products help prevent blood sugar levels from soaring too quickly.

The components of the date point to the possibility that it can prevent cancer. Our living proof is the low rate of cancer among populations where dates are regularly consumed. It is also said to slow ageing. The longevity of many Bedouins of the desert might have something to do with their date-focused diet. Dates are rich in carbohydrates, calcium, potassium and magnesium. The pollen has been found to yield an oestrogenic principle that boosts libido and activates milk hormones. It has also been discovered that dates act as a tonic for the uterine muscles, thus stimulating delivery contractions. They may also prevent post-delivery bleeding. Dates are nowadays believed to allay anxiety and nervous disorders in children: seven dates a day will do it. Eating dates is said to be good for haemorrhoids, and beneficial in treating alcoholism in a natural way that minimizes the urge for alcohol. All it takes is drinking the liquid in which a few dates have been steeped for a couple of hours, twice a day for one month. Worth trying, isn't it?

4

The Eminent History of the Date

Like a thread of peaceful, life-giving green, the concern with this tree and its cultivation runs through the almost six thousand years of a history that was as distinguished and fascinating as it was turbulent and beset by wars and violence.

Hilda Simon, *The Date Palm: Bread of the Desert*

Ancient Mesopotamia

The green line, to adopt Simon's metaphor, begins with the cradle of civilization. The earliest evidence of date palm cultivation, from 4000 BC, comes from Ur, lower Mesopotamia, where it played a predominant role in Sumerian economic life. The temple of the moon god itself was constructed from its trunks. From lexicographical lists from the early second millennium BC, we learn of about 150 words for the various types of the palm and its different parts. When Herodotus visited Babylonia in the fifth century BC, he was fascinated by the sight of the date palms. Such a beautiful and generous tree that imposed itself upon the ancient scene was bound to play a central role in its people's spiritual and religious rituals.

Agate cylinder seal engraved with a scene showing the Persian king Darius I (reigned 521–486 BC) standing in a chariot and shooting arrows at lions. The scene is framed by date palms. The cuneiform inscription written along one side is in three languages – Old Persian, Elamite and Babylonian – and translates as 'Darius the great king'.

An impression of a third-millennium BC Akkadian cylinder seal at the British Museum shows a female figure sitting on a chair facing a male figure (a god, as identified by his horned headdress), with a date palm standing between them, and a serpent in the background undulating upwards. This scene suggested to some the temptation story of Adam and Eve in the Garden of Eden but others see this as no more than a worshipper facing her god, and the date palm and the serpent as symbols of fertility. Whether Garden of Eden or worship act, the scene significantly depicts the date palm as an important tree worthy of being included in sacred rituals.

The date palm was seen as a divine gift, which possessed a special power. Dates were offered at marriage ceremonies as a symbol of plenty and fecundity, and fronds were used during magic ceremonies to protect from evil. The sorcerer would trace a circle around himself and whomever he was protecting with the words, 'In my hand I hold the magic circle of Ea, in my hand I hold the cedar wood, the sacred weapon of Ea, in my hand I hold the branch of the palm tree of the great rite.'[1]

The date palm was their livelihood, and cutting it down was a crime punishable by law. According to Hammurabi's law, 'If a landlord cut down a tree in another landlord's orchard without the consent of the owner of the orchard, he shall pay one-half *mina* of silver [approx. 10 oz/285 g].' And yet the date palms of the conquered in times of war were cut down. A Sumerian text entitled *Lament of Sumer* describes how they were destroyed in vengeance:

> The palm-trees, strong as mighty copper, the heroic strength, were torn out like rushes, were plucked like rushes, their trunks were turned sideways. Their tops lay in the dust, there was no one to raise them. The midribs of their palm fronds were cut off and their tops were burnt off. Their date spadices were torn out.[2]

The aim of the enemy was no doubt to depopulate the city and prevent people from resettling.

According to a Sumerian legend, the date palm was the first fruit tree created on earth. The myth tells how in the city of Eridu in southern Mesopotamia, Enki (Akkadian Ea), god of the freshwater ocean, created the date palm with the help of Inanna (Akkadian Ishtar) and a raven. The raven performed actions which would be allotted to man, such as climbing the palm and pollinating it, and using the *shaduf* to irrigate the date palm grove.

It is not surprising then that the date palm in Mesopotamia was one of the most ancient symbolic forms of the concept of the 'Tree of Life', the sacred tree that connects heaven, earth and the underworld, and is the giver of gifts: wisdom, immortality and fertility.

Assyrian soldiers cutting down an enemy's palm trees south of Babylon.
Drawing of a lost sculpture in the palace of Assyrian King Sennacherib
(705–681 BC), by Austin Layard, *Monuments of Nineveh* (1853).

Wherever the palm grew, it fascinated people with its
beauty and utility. The mythical deification of the date palm as
the tree of life is not unique to Mesopotamia. Myths related
to Nigeria's Yoruba people tell the story of a great god who
looked down and saw the world beneath him as only a vast
sea. He sent his sons down to start creating the earth. As they
descended, he lowered a great palm tree that settled on the
waters. The brothers landed on the leaves and almost at once
one of the sons began hacking at the bark and made a strong
palm wine from the sap. He got intoxicated and fell asleep,
while the other son went down and established the world.[3]

Ancient Egypt

When Herodotus visited Babylonia in the middle of the fifth century BC, he raved about the date palms he saw there. Not so when he went to Egypt, but he mentioned the palm wine used in mummification. Still, from abundant archaeological and architectural evidence we know that the date palm was grown and revered in the western Saharan oases and along the Nile Valley from early times, perhaps simultaneously with Near Eastern countries in Asia. However, the culture of the date palm did not become important until the third and second millennia BC. Many pictorial records from the Nile region depict the date palm. The third-millennium BC granite temple pillars of King Sahure at Abuseer were shaped like date palms, and bas relief sculptures and paintings illustrate stages of palm cultivation. A carving from the kingdom of Memphis shows a priest irrigating palms, and in decorations on tomb walls, date palms are shown as growing around rectangular pools.

The date palm was the abode and emblem of several deities. As a symbol of femininity, it was associated with goddess Hathor, the counterpart of the Mesopotamian Ishtar, goddess of life, joy, music, dancing and fertility. The date palm was also depicted as the abode of goddess Nephtys, who offered dates and water to the deceased.

The Egyptians used the leaves as a symbol of longevity and fertility. The god of infinity, Heh, was often shown holding two palm midribs symbolic of the passage of time. In temples the midribs were notched to record the cycle of time.

Ancient Judaism

Among the ancient Jews, the date palm had a special place. It featured prominently on the decorated gilded walls and doors of Solomon's temple, 'within and without'.[4] In the Psalms, the righteous are said to flourish like the date palm.[5] It is also invoked in one of the enchanting love songs of Solomon:

> How fair and how pleasant art thou, O love, for delights!
> This thy stature is like to a palm tree, and thy breasts to
>   clusters of grapes.
> I said, I will go up to the palm tree, I will take hold of the
>   boughs thereof.[6]

In the book of Genesis, the Tree of Life in the midst of the garden is understood by most to be a date palm.[7] It is mentioned once again in the last chapter of the Book of Revelation, 'And on either side of the river, was there the tree of life, which bare twelve manner of fruits, and yielded her fruit every month: and the leaves of the tree were for the healing of the nations.'[8] The symbolic significance of the number twelve lies in the belief that 'the palm tree was popularly believed to put forth a shoot every month, and hence became, at the close of the year, a symbol of it; and was the origin of the Christmas tree'.[9] This ultimately drew on the ancient Egyptian notion that the trunk stands for 'year' and the leaves for 'months'.

Like the ancient Egyptians, Jews carried palm branches during festivals. It was the symbol of the Kingdom of Judea, as a provider of food, shelter and shade. In the Old Testament, the land of 'milk and honey' was the land of Canaan located on the banks of the Jordan River, where date palms and date honey were abundant. In the Psalms of David the righteous are promised prosperity 'like the palm tree'. Jericho was described as 'the city of palm trees'.

The palm tree featured on Hebrew coins, as well as Phoenician and Carthaginian ones. To commemorate the conquering of the Jews and the destruction of Jerusalem by Titus, a new, special bronze coin called 'Judaea Capta' was minted. It showed the Jewish state as a weeping woman beneath a date palm. Palm tree images were also struck on Greek and Roman coins. All this emphasizes the importance of the tree as an economic resource, and reveals that the date palm left its stamp even in places where palm trees were not traditional or native.

Classical Antiquity

Greeks and Romans loved the date palm as a decorative motif, and depicted it especially in mosaics. The tall Greek marble columns with their curling bushy tops are evocative of it. The date palm was associated with their chief god, Apollo. In the *Odyssey*, Ulysses compares Nausicaa to a palm he once saw on the altar of Apollo in the temple of Delos:

> Never, I never viewed till this blest hour
> Such finished grace! I gaze, and I adore!
> Thus seems the palm, which stately honors crowned
> By Phoebes alters; thus overlooks the ground;
> The pride of Delos.[10]

In Greek myths, Apollo and his twin sister Artemis were born under a palm tree. The Delian palm gained increasing significance, as the island became the resort of Apollo's pilgrims.

Roman mosaic of a date palm in the pavement of the main sanctuary, Synagogue of Hammam-Lif, Tunisia, third to fifth century AD.

Tourists' hotel in Palmyra, Syria, at the very edge of the ruins of the Roman era. The tall Roman columns were sculpted to look like date palms.

The ancient Greeks and Romans adopted the palm leaves as symbols for victory, worn by champions of games or military leaders as wreaths or carried by hand. Whereas some scholars trace such customs to Semitic origins, others argue that the sacredness of the palm fronds is more related to the myth of Heracles. The date palm was the first thing he saw on his return from the netherworld, and he crowned himself with its leaves.

Christianity

Christians use the palm branch to symbolize the victory of the faithful, as on Palm Sunday. It all started when Jesus entered Jerusalem as a victor and his followers greeted him with palm fronds, as was the custom in the region at the time. Soon enough, the Christan church adopted the palm frond as a symbol for victory and martyrdom, which led to the planting of large palm groves in Italy to supply Rome with palm fronds for Easter ceremonies. More expensive and much prized were the white fronds, which gradually gained in popularity. Today, from about the middle of summer, the leaves of the palms are tied together in a bunch so that the inner ones gradually lose their greenness and turn white due to lack of chlorophyll. The Spanish groves in Elche, which grow sweet edible date palms, are also a source of these peculiar leaves. The white frond became a symbol of heavenly purity in addition to the already inherited meaning as an ancient pagan symbol of victory.

To this day Elche is famous for its annual festival, known as the Pilgrimage to Elche. One of the activities included is a medieval miracle play featuring the death and ascension of Mary. It begins with an angel descending in a golden cloud shaped like a date palm to the aged Mary. The angel carries a golden palm frond, which he hands to her with the explanation that from it a date palm will grow on her grave.

Islamic Lore

To Muslims, the date palm and its fruit was a God-sent gift, a miracle food capable of healing body and soul. According to a famous saying by the Prophet, 'A house empty of dates is a poor house indeed.' It was their livelihood and Tree of Life. The forbidden tree in paradise was said to be a date palm. It is repeatedly mentioned in the Qur'an as a token of God's bounty to his creatures. In one of the verses, a beneficent word is compared to a beneficent tree with roots deep in earth and head high up in heaven.

In the story of the miraculous birth of Jesus in the Qur'an, Mary was to shake the trunk of the date palm so that she might eat the falling dates. The miracle here is not only having the strength to shake the trunk, but also a date palm carrying fresh dates in winter.

A saying by the Prophet urges Muslims to honour the palm, for it is their paternal aunt. It is Adam's sister. According to Muslim lore, the date palm was created from what was left of Adam's clay. When the angel appeared to Adam after the creation, he said to him, 'You were created of the same material as this tree which shall nourish you.' The analogy between humans and the palm is elaborated on. It stands upright, the sexes are separate, it needs to be pollinated by the male to produce, the pollen itself is said to smell like semen. If its head is cut off, it dies; and if its fronds are cut off, it cannot grow new ones in the same place. Adam is described by the Prophet as a tall man with lots of hair on his head, like a tall date palm.

Circulated legends tell how the date palms were honoured and moved by the presence of the Prophet. Once a date palm bent its head and said, 'Peace be upon you', when he ate from its fruit. The mosque in which the Prophet was buried was the first Islamic mosque built in Medina after he and his followers migrated to it. It was built mostly of palm trunks and fronds. The first *muezzin*, Bilal, used to climb palm trees to call the faithful to prayers five times a day. The Islamic minaret was inspired by the date palm.

When the Arabs ruled Andalusia for almost eight centuries, they spread their love and knowledge of the date palm to many regions in Spain and Italy, climate permitting. The tree became their identifier. When in the fifteenth century the Arabs were expelled from Spain, the palms were almost completely exterminated by the Christians, who uprooted them as they were looked upon as the relics of the non-believers. Only the date palm groves of Elche in southern Spain escaped the ravages of politics and religion.

Tree of Love

To the Arab mind, the date palm is perfection itself, and its beauty and utility never ceased to fascinate. Aside from religious writings, the tree prominently featured in their *belles lettres* and folklore. A couple of didactic verses advise:

> Rise above ignobility and be like the date palm.
> When stones are thrown at it, it retaliates with sweet dates.

Being on top of the date palm is a common metaphor for glory, and the coveted unattainable. Since goodly appearances can sometimes be deceptive, an impressively attractive person with no real substance is said to be as tall as a date palm with the brain of a goat. A beautiful anonymous Arabic poem was freely translated into English in the nineteenth

A wall mosaic on the Treasury of the Umayyad Mosque in Damascus, Syria. The revered date palm was deemed worthy of being featured on a mosque wall.

century by Bayard Taylor, whose imaginative rendition com-
plemented the poet's infatuation with the palm:

> Next to thee, O fair Gazelle!
> O Bedowee girl, beloved so well,
> Next to the fearless Nejidee,
> Whose fleetness shall bear me again to thee –
> Next to ye both I love the palm
> With his leaves of beauty and fruit of balm.
> Next to ye both, I love the tree,
> Whose fluttering shadows wrap us three.
> In love and silence and mystery.
> The noble minarets that begem
> Cairo's citadel diadem
> Are not so light as his slender stem.
> He lifts his leaves in the sunbeam glance
> As the Almehs lift their arms in dance;
> A slumberous motion, a passionate sigh
> That works in the cells of the blood like wine.
> O tree of love, by that love of thine
> Teach me how I shall soften mine.[11]

When the American writer Mark Twain was asked to describe the date palm, he said it looked like a liberty pole with
a haycock on top of it.

Celebrating the Date

It used to be that the seasons for harvesting the dates and
pollinating them were big occasions for celebrations and
revelries. In ancient Mesopotamia, for instance, springtime
was a big time for New Year festivities, during which the

Date palm grove, perfect setting for the story of the woeful lovers Layla and Qays, as depicted in a *Khamsa* miniature by Nizami (1462). It is based on the famous story of the 7th-century star-crossed Arabian lovers Layla and Qays, who both died very young. Sad Layla is shown sitting in the background, and the distraught Qays is being comforted by his only friend Salim and the peaceful animals around them. After Layla's father prohibited their marriage, Qays lost his mind and people started calling him Majnun (lunatic).

ritualistic marriage between Ishtar, patron of the date palm, and the ruling king was performed to bless the crops. Of the rare places where the date harvest is still celebrated like in the old days is the Tibesti village at the borders between south Libya and northern Chad. A largely isolated Muslim tribe of Teda lives there, to whom date palm cultivation still plays an important role. The highlight of the year is the date festival, held early in the autumn. They celebrate it with marriages, circumcisions, dancing around date palms and carousing on date wine.

It is more common in the Middle East to use the palm in social celebrations. During wedding ceremonies in Bahrain, for instance, people decorate the entrance of the house with palm leaves, as they indicate this happy occasion and bring blessings to the newlywed couples. In Oman people still plant a date palm offshoot for every newborn son, following the old tradition. Date festivals in the Gulf countries have started to take place in recent years, mostly to encourage farmers by arranging competitions and distributing prizes for the best date.

Ironically, for the largest date celebration today we have to go to the New World. Every February the National Date

Festive stuffed dates (for recipe, see pp. 114–15).

'Picking Dates in a Palm Grove', by a 14-year-old Saudi girl (1995),
a winner in a nationwide contest held annually in Dhahran, Saudi Arabia.

A flier for the year 2000 National Date Festival held annually in Indio, Coachella Valley, southern California.

Festival is held in Indio in the Coachella Valley in southern California. A 2004 announcement for the festival reads:

> A scene out of the Arabian nights, the National Date Festival and Riverside County Fair is held each year in date-crazed Indio. There are camel and ostrich races, an Arabian Nights Pageant outdoor musical, the Blessing of the Dates Ceremony, and more Middle Eastern appreciation than you'll find in the whole rest of the USA.[12]

5
Looking for the Date:
A Bird's-Eye View

It will be with very fair reason, then that we shall confine our
description to the palm-tree of foreign countries . . . It is only in
the hottest climates that this tree will bear fruit.
Pliny the Elder, *Natural History*

To find the date we have to go to regions where summer is
long and dry. Although the tree can tolerate long periods of
drought, its legendary heavy-bearing harvest needs plenty of
water for the roots, the source of which is not rain but irrigation water. The most suitable soil for its growth is sand and
sandy loam (a mixture of sand, clay, silt and organic matter),
which provide an excellent medium for aeration and drainage.
It is remarkably tolerant of alkaline soil.

The climate requirements for growing date palms given
above make it sound as though it is an easy-going tree, which
in a way is true. However, it is rather more demanding to
grow the tree as a profitable commercial commodity. According to date experts, the ideal combination of moisture and
temperature is 'extremely difficult to find and limits date cultivation to a very few places on the face of earth'.[1] Give it
extreme heat and extended periods of drought, and the dates
will come out hard and mummified and will have no chance

of ripening to the *rutab* stage. Give it extreme heat – which it actually likes – coupled with humidity as in coastal areas, and the dates will ferment or rot and fall before they reach the final *tamr* stage. Give it cool temperatures, and the fruit will have no chance of ripening. The perfect conditions are to keep the roots well watered – there is no such thing as over-watering the date palm – and the growing fruit dry and hot.

The date palm is an old Old World tree. It is not known exactly when and where the date palm originated, but fossils from around 50 million years ago were found in the Fertile Crescent region. Evidently, it was grown throughout North Africa and western and southwestern Asia to the Indus valley. Its cultivation coincided with the oldest civilizations, the most important centres of which were ancient Mesopotamia and Egypt. Ancient Carthage and the Arabian Peninsula were also great date centres.

The consensus seems to be that the date palm 'was first brought into cultivation somewhere in the lower Mesopotamian basin, which happened around the fifth millennium BC'.[2] From there, the cultivated date palm with all the accumulated agricultural knowledge and techniques gradually spread to the surrounding regions all the way to northwestern Africa and the Indus valley eastwards.

Dates were eaten in the Indus valley from early times but it is believed that the Indians already had trade contacts with Mesopotamia and they might have imported the date from there. Another venue for the migrating dates to north India might have originated from the thousands of date stones spat by Alexander's soldiers around their camps there. The nutritious and handy dried dates of Mesopotamia were part of the soldiers' rations.

Ancient Greeks and Romans of antiquity were fond of the date fruit. They used it in cooking, decorated their boulevards

A sweet treat for the next life in a basket woven from date palm fronds. Dried dates can be seen among other fruits such as pomegranate and sycomore figs (Arabic *jummayz*). Egypt, 18th Dynasty (1550–1295 BC).

with it, and knew a lot about it. The places where it grew were part of their eastern empire. From Theophrastus' observations in the third century BC, we learn how the palm was planted and propagated. It is 'very fond of irrigation', he writes, but 'requires spring water rather than water from the skies'. He mentions instances where the palm grew in Europe, such as Cyprus, where the dates do not ripen but stay green, still tasting sweet and luscious. Of the other places where the palm grew, he mentions Syria, Arabia and Egypt.[3]

Pliny comments that palms were 'not uncommon in Italy, but are quite barren there', since it is only 'in the hottest climates that this tree will bear fruit'. In Arabia, he says, the fruit is 'sickly sweet', but praises the dates of Judea. The fresh ones have a rich taste, their juice 'unctuous' and of 'milky consistency, and have a sort of vinous flavour with a remarkable sweetness, like that of honey'. The dates of Arabia and

Thebes he says are dry and small with a shrivelled body, since they are parched and scorched by the constant heat.[4]

Today the central zone of commercial cultivation of the date palm in the Old World remains in the traditional areas. Of the main producing countries, Iraq used to top the list, but not any more. Apart from the northern region, the date palm grows everywhere it can be irrigated by water of the Tigris and Euphrates and their tributaries. It is more concentrated in Basra around Shatt al-'Arab river, which is the confluent of the Tigris and Euphrates. The weather is warmer there and irrigation is naturally regulated by the ebb and flow of the river's water, which is open to the Arabian Gulf, a perfect natural irrigation system not found anywhere else in the date palm growing regions worldwide. Up until the 1990s Iraq was at the top of the date producing and exporting countries. The sanctions imposed on the country after the invasion of Kuwait, and the ensuing ravaging wars, political instability and lack of security, combined with a lack of modern farming equipment, crippled the industry. Even a simple task like climbing the tree to pollinate or harvest the dates became a life-threatening experience because the climbers might easily be mistaken for snipers. Nonetheless, in terms of the quality of the varieties that grow there, Iraq is still the champion producer. The farmers' explanation is that it is the water of the two rivers.

Growing dates in the Arabian Peninsula has a long tradition. The concentration of date palms is in the western province of Saudi Arabia, and the eastern regions of the peninsula. They are all irrigated by underground water, springs and *aflaj* canals (singular *falaj*). *Aflaj* is the principal irrigation system used in Oman to supply the date palm groves with the needed water. The source of the water is mostly a deep well or rainwater reservoirs. Many of the canals were built by 500 BC.

Iraqi coins featuring the national tree of the country.

Iraqi 50-dinar bill featuring a date palm grove.

In Saudi Arabia date palm cultivation is centred in the oases, such as Hasa and Qateef in the eastern Province, Qaseem in the central province and Medina in the west. Of the eastern Arabian region, Bahrain's dates were famous in the ancient world. Bahrain was called Dilmun, and a Sumerian text described it as a 'pleasant dwelling place', whose dates are 'very big'.[5] In Iran date palms grow in the southwest regions, where climate is similar to that of southern Iraq. Date production there got a devastating blow during the Iran-Iraq war in the 1980s.

In northeast and east-central Pakistan and northwest India the domesticated date palms grow inferior fruit because they were originally propagated from seedlings. Most of the dates are domestically consumed, especially during religious festivals. The climate there is rather tricky, especially during the ripening season, due to humidity and unpredictable monsoon rains. Northwest India is the eastern limit of the global distribution of the date palm.

In China dates are known and consumed, but the tree does not grow there. The Chinese imported dates from Persia from early times. So-called Chinese dates are not dates but dried jujube (*Ziziphus vulgaris*). One of the Chinese names for dates is 'jujube from Persia'. Attempts to grow the date palm in China in medieval times were not successful.[6]

In the Levant, Jordan's production of the dates is marginal, and in Syria date growth is centred in its desert oases such as

'*Hurriya*' (freedom, also a woman's name), oil painting by Iraqi artist Maysaloon Faraj, 2004. From her collection *Boats and Burdens: Kites and Shattered Dreams*, which she dedicates to 'the women of Iraq, who despite burden upon unprecedented burden stand tall, proud, and resilient, like their precious date palms'.

Date palm grove in Wadi Dayqa in Oman, irrigated by *falaj*, a canal system whose source of water is mostly a deep well or a rain-water reservoir.

in Palmyra, but it is hardly enough for domestic consumption. Palestine is struggling to build an economically feasible date industry in the Jordan Valley and Gaza Strip, and its biggest asset is the expertise of the Arab farmers. But the major obstacle is Israeli control of fundamental resources, land, water, market and borders. Israel seems to be doing well enough even though growing dates there started late. In ancient times Judea was renowned for its dates, but nothing remained of the palms by the nineteenth century. Cultivating them anew in the upper Jordan valley took place in 1924 when many varieties were imported directly from Iraq and Egypt, and North African ones were brought directly from California. They were all grown in kibbutzim and cooperative villages. Today, the date of preference is *medjool*, with an eye on export. Consumption of dates in Israel is low.

Saudi one-guinea gold coin, issued in 1957. It depicts the country's national emblem adopted in 1950, two crossed swords and a date palm in the middle, which is said to symbolize vitality, progress and welfare.

In Egypt the majority of the date palms are widely scattered over the Nile valley, from north of Cairo to Aswan in Upper Egypt. However, due to dry weather and the fact that most of the palms were grown from seeds, the dates are dry and of inferior quality. The western region consists of a desert land with many oases. The area is famous for a propagated variety called *saidi* (variant on *sa'eedi* 'from Upper Egypt'). The Nile delta is not hot enough and is relatively humid. Therefore, most of the dates grown there are high in moisture, and have to be eaten fresh within days; otherwise they rot. They satisfy the domestic demand while in season. Off season, the indigenous dry dates are eked out with imports. The date growing region in Sudan is an extension to that of southern Egypt. The date makes the bulk of the income and food there. Due to the excessively hot and dry weather, most varieties are of dry, inferior types. To make things worse, date production has deteriorated in the last two decades due to fluctuations in climate, drought, flooding and the spread of insect pests and plant diseases.

The Sahara in northern Africa is a different story. The Saharan oases of Tripoli, Tunisia and Algeria grow many good varieties, such as *deglet noor*. Both Algeria and Tunisia have the lion's share of exporting this variety to Europe. Morocco grows good dates in the Tafilalet oases, where the huge date variety *medjool* originated. Recent reports, however, warn that the beautiful Moroccan date palm oases are being threatened by desertification.

In the northern shores of the Mediterranean Sea of today, the only place where the tree has been successful is a small pocket in Spain. It is Elche, 'The City of Palms' in the south-eastern province of Alicante. The groves were first planted by the ancient Carthaginians of North Africa who themselves were great growers of the date palm. The palms were planted at the request of the Romans, whose ultimate purpose was to provide a dam against the periodical flooding by the high tidal waves. Fruit production was of a secondary consideration. During the Arab rule in Andalusia, date palm cultivation was much improved. Alicante today is famous in Europe for its date wine and syrup known as *mile de Elche* 'honey of Elche'.

Around the beginning of the twentieth century, there were attempts to improve the quality of dates at regions where the trees were grown from seedlings by introducing offshoots, such as in Punjab. There was also interest in spreading or improving the cultivation of the tree in other African regions located in the southern hemisphere of the globe so that the world may have year round supply of dates. The arid regions of Namibia, for instance, already have local varieties of dates, which were originally propagated from seeds about four centuries ago. They grow in geographic isolation. Commercial growth was not possible due to lack of technical knowledge. However, in the last two decades or so, there have

Date palm grove in Alice Springs, Northern Territory in Australia,
early 20th century. Date palms being irrigated by flooding with water.

been attempts to improve the industry. Namibia started to
produce *medjool*, and it now runs a tissue culture centre.

In Australia the date palm was introduced to the Alice
Springs region in the Northern Territory, and more recently
in the Western region, where production is still local. The
incentive in recent years has been the increasing demand for
the date due to the increased migration from Muslim countries, where consuming dates is an established religious custom. Many date varieties are available, but their cultivation is
still costly. Therefore, most of the demand for dates is met
by import.

As for the Americas, the tree was introduced to north-
eastern Argentina, Brazil, Chile and Peru, but on a small scale.
For a more significant date production, we have to go further
north.

The Assiduous Immigrant
of the Western World

'Palm trees don't belong here, you know.
They've been planted over the decades by
immigrants. Spaniards, Iraqis, Egyptians.'
'Spider Palm', a short story by Rodger Jacobs[7]

Americans love to romanticize the date palm. If you happen to visit Coachella Valley in southern California, the homeland of the immigrant date, a visit to Shields along Highway 111, nicknamed the Date Palm Highway, is in order. A large banner of a knight ushers you into the store, and a yellow one promises a free show of 'The Romance and Sex Life of the Date'. And that is only one of many date stores along the road.

About 95 per cent of US palms grow in Coachella Valley, and the rest in Yuma, Arizona, and other smaller pockets. The capital of the date in California is Indio, where the annual National Date Festival takes place.

The pioneers of the date industry in the United States were certainly not individual Spaniards, Iraqis and Egyptian immigrants, as the short story quoted above states. They might have planted date palms here and there from seeds of dates they brought from home, but seeds, with their 50/50 chance of growing into males and with unpredictable varieties, do not an industry make. Still, that was how the date palm itself was first introduced to the Western Hemisphere centuries ago on the western shores of Mexico and southern California. It all began soon after Columbus' expeditions in the Americas, with the Spanish explorers and missionaries, who were quite familiar with the date and the religious significance of the tree's fronds.

Highway 111, also known as the 'Date Palm Highway', in Coachella Valley, southern California, along which are located date palm groves and date shops.

The earliest available records tell that the first attempts at establishing date palm plantations were in Cuba in 1513. Both date palms and tobacco were introduced. Whereas tobacco flourished, the date palms did not like the climate there, as it was too humid. All that remains of them today is the name of the city El Datil, a Spanish word for 'date'.[8]

As the Spaniards moved northwards through Mexico and up to California along the shores they carried date palm seedlings and seeds. They left a trail of date palms, which did not really grow dates, and if they did, they never ripened well because climate was too humid. Some of the palms had a better chance in the drier regions in the interior of Mexico and southern California and Arizona. They were mostly planted by Spanish missionaries. By the middle of the nineteenth century, the relative success of growing them from seedlings, which was made possible by the availability of underground water resources in the area, caught the attention of some experts of the US Department of Agriculture, who were a small group of 'imaginative and enterprising men'.[9] In the beginning, they tried with seedlings, many of them. But they did not see any possible future for commercial growth this way.

Therefore many attempts were made to import offshoots from date-growing Arab countries. They tried with Algeria, Egypt and Oman first, but the offshoots were not of good quality and the enterprise was doomed to failure. The earliest successful imported offshoots were mostly *deglet noor* from Algeria. This took place around the turn of the twentieth century. Then, a succession of importations followed, made possible by the pioneering Government horticulturists, who were driven by their curiosity and adventurous spirits at a time when it was not safe for foreigners to go beyond the cosmopolitan centres in the Arab world. Once brought to the US, the imported offshoots were quarantined at first and then implanted at experimental stations in New Mexico, Arizona and California.

Between 1901 and 1905 important offshoot varieties were obtained from Iraq, Egypt, Algeria and Tunisia. In 1912 another round of importation was undertaken, this time by Paul Popenoe, who knew his date very well. His book *Date Growing in the Old World and the New* (1913) is a classic in the field. He secured offshoots for many good varieties: *deglet noor* from Algeria, *fard* from Oman, a good number of *Khalasa* from Hasa in Arabia, *Barhi*, *khadrawi*, and *halawi* (*hillawi*) from Basra, and *zahidi* (*zahdi*) from Baghdad. Most of the trees he brought proved to be quite successful. At the beginning of 1920s, *saidi* and *hayani* varieties were imported from Egypt.

In 1927 an important date was introduced to the US by chance. The story goes that the date industry in Morocco was suffering seriously from major attacks of the bayoud disease, which threatened to destroy all the date palms. Swingle, the American date expert, was invited to help in the situation. While there, he managed to get 11 offshoots of *medjool* dates, which happened to be free of the disease. They were first planted in southern Nevada to make sure they were not infected. While there, a dog dug out and destroyed two of them. In 1935 the remaining nine offshoots were transplanted to the Government experimental station in Indio, where they grew and flourished. Their offshoots were distributed to commercial date growers, beginning in 1944, and *medjool* rapidly

In southern California today, mature date palms are in great demand for landscaping, as in this shopping strip mall in Indio, Coachella Valley. The trees are usually left unfertilized.

established itself as the major date in America. Thus the surviving nine offshoots saved the *medjool* date for the world.

The experimental phase ended with the last importation from Iraq in 1929, and the focus shifted to taking care of and propagating the varieties which had already proved to have a future. Meanwhile, the increasing success of the government enterprise encouraged commercial production by private date growers.

Not all imported varieties adjusted well to their new home. At the beginning, many offshoots died due to lack of experience and traditions in taking care of the trees. Nonetheless, many investors believed that the date palm had an unlimited future and were not ready to give up on it, even though it was clear to all it was not a get-rich-quick type of business. Therefore, to save the industry, a lot of research was done, books were written and field trips were repeatedly undertaken to the original home of the date. Along the road, they solved many problems related to the date's growth, processing and packaging, and many machines were devised and gadgets invented to meet the challenge, to the extent that the New World was in a position to benefit the Old World with the knowledge they had gained.

In the 1940s water from the Colorado River was brought to Coachella valley and the surrounding areas, and the date industry flourished. It was also a profitable time for the growers because the Government purchased large amounts of dates to distribute them to the World War II troops. The industry reached its zenith in the 1960s.

For the last two decades or so, there seems to have been rising demand not for the date but for the trees themselves, as mature palms for landscaping. This 'was a boon to many older date farmers, ready to retire, and to others', Patricia Laflin, the date historian, explains, 'who did not want to continue farming the tall trees with the resultant higher costs and dangers to workers.'[10]

During my visit to Coachella valley last summer, I heard people bemoaning the fact that real estate is now more valuable than date palms, and I saw many areas with neglected palms and palm trunk stubs waiting for their turn to be overhauled by the developers.

6

The Future of the Date

The date, mostly dried, is today a global fruit thanks to advanced technology in transportation and refrigeration and the increasing awareness of its goodness. Another factor is the significant number of immigrants from the Middle East as well as other Asian countries who are scattered all over the world. They are predominantly Muslims, and consuming dates is traditional in their native countries.

As an alternative to importation, many countries have been experimenting with growing the date palm, with the result that it has already spread to five continents, with the centre of growth still in the Middle East as of old. The good news is that in the last few decades, tissue culture technology has seen considerable progress and proven to be quite successful in mass-producing desirable varieties of date palms at reasonable cost, although it is still not economical by some standards. The resulting trees grow 30 per cent faster than traditionally reared palms. The tissue-cultured plants are easier to transport and do not fall under the governments' imposed quarantine regulations because they are free of diseases. A number of laboratories for producing tissue-cultured palms are functioning today in places like North Africa, Saudi Arabia and the rest of the Gulf countries, and southern Africa, as in

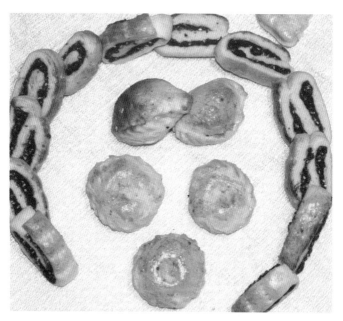

Date-filled cookies (for recipe, see pp. 119–20).

Namibia. *Medjool* tops the list of tissue-cultured varieties. It has become the super-date of our modern age.

The date is a high-calorie, nourishing food that can be used effectively to fight global hunger. It can be conveniently transported when dried as it needs no refrigeration and seldom harbours bacteria. It truly is the 'cake of the poor'. Given man's natural propensity to sweet foods, it is more likely to be the most palatable item in the food-rescue packages dispatched in humanitarian efforts to fight hunger, which more often than not happens in arid areas where people are more familiar with dates than with peanut butter, for instance. An amusing newspaper article I read a few years ago tells how an Afghan villager was puzzled by the peanut butter included in the American food aid packets dropped on them. He tasted

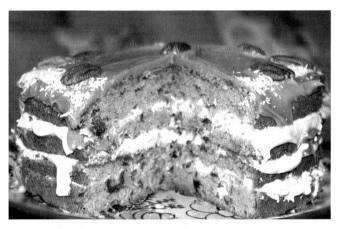

Spicy date cake (for recipe, see pp. 121 2).

it but did not like it, so he gave it to his donkey. The donkey refused to eat it.

An endless number of proposed projects to use the date in commercial products are now on the table. They range from manufacturing baker's yeast from date syrup, to using dates as a replacement for wheat in brewing soy sauce, incorporating them into carbonated beverages, milk products, frozen desserts and chutneys, or making them part of meals for school-age children.

As for the secondary products of date palms, such as light furniture and basketry, these are not going anywhere. They are still as practical and useful as ever. When modern technology failed in Iraq during the ravaging times of war, what came to the rescue in the scorching months of summer were the millennia-old handheld fans made of woven date palm fronds.

The most exciting news about the date by far is that it can be the fuel of the future. According to recent reports, soon our cars may be powered with an eco-friendly bio-fuel as an alternative to the traditional fossil fuel, oil. A name has already been coined for it: *Nakhoil*, a combination of the Arabic *nakhl* (date palm) and oil.

The buzz started in 2007 at the spread of the news that an Omani entrepreneur had plans to make the Omani Sultanate the first Arab country to produce an alternative to petrol if he was allowed to have his way. His way was to tap the sucrose-rich sap of the date palm to produce fuel ethanol. To those who know the date palm well enough, this project had the word failure written all over it because tapping *Phoenix dactylifera* means its end.

More feasible, though, is the recent news that bio-fuel can be produced from the enormous amounts of dates which go to waste every year in the Arab world.[1] In addition to being environmentally clean, this industry will encourage the planting of more date palms. This will further serve the environment by checking the spread of desertification, which in turn will reduce heat and combat global warming.

Recipes

A good housewife may furnish her husband every day for a
month with a dish of dates differently prepared.

Arab proverb

To enjoy dates, you do not really need a recipe. Simply eat them as
a snack with a glass of milk, buttermilk, whipped diluted plain
yoghurt or sugarless coffee. They pair very well with cucumbers
(the small tender ones). In the Arab Gulf region choice dates are
customarily offered to guests with Arabian coffee. A traditional
Arabian treat would be dried dates stuffed with clotted cream
(*qaymer/qishta*), which can be replaced with cream cheese or ricotta.
Dates can also be stuffed with nuts; in the West these are enjoyed
as a Christmas treat. Or just chop them and sprinkle them over
your salad or cereal.

Historical Recipes

Date Syrup (*Dibs*)

The thirteenth-century Arab botanist Ibn al-Baytar describes how
date syrup is made. According to the cold press method, called
sayalan (oozing), a weight is put on the dried soft dates to let syrup
ooze out naturally. The boiling method uses equal amounts of

dates and boiling water, which are cooked together until the dates disintegrate. Then the mixture is beaten, strained and put in big containers in the sun to thicken, if it is made in summertime. In winter the strained mixture is returned to the pot to boil down to the desired consistency. Date syrup is still prepared the same way.

Iraqi Jews call date syrup *silan*, and use it to prepare the traditional *haroseth*, one of the Seder dishes for Passover. Date syrup is mixed with chopped walnuts until it looks lumpy and pasty. Date syrup is traditionally served with clotted cream (*geymer/qishta*) and warm bread. It makes a delicious winter dip when generously drizzled with *tahini*, sesame paste.

Honeyed Dates (*Rutab Mu'assal*)
— Date jam recipe from al-Baghdadi's thirteenth-century cookbook

Take completely ripe fresh dates (*rutab*), and spread them in a shady ventilated place for a day. Remove the seeds and replace them with skinned almonds. Then, for every ten *ratls* (10 lb/4½ kg) of dates, take two *ratls* (2 lb/900 g) of honey. Let them boil over the fire with two *uqiyyas* (2 oz/60 g) of rose water and half a *dirham* (1½ g) of saffron. Then throw in the dates, and let them boil while stirring, for an hour. Remove the pot and let it cool off. When cool enough, sprinkle with finely ground sugar, which has been scented with musk, camphor and spikenard. Empty the jam into glass jars, and sprinkle the top with some of the scented ground sugar. Cover the jars and do not open them until wintertime. (my translation)

Date Wine (*Nabeedh al-Tamr*)

In medieval Baghdad, a variety of date wine was made with an additive called *dadhi*, a mysterious ingredient, which might have been hops or wormwood, or even stronger stuff like marijuana and datura/thorn apple. It was added to preserve the wine, but also to make it more potent. Here is a tenth-century wine recipe from Ibn Sayyar al-Warraq's cookbook, which uses date syrup (*dibs*).

Take fifty *ratls* (50 lb/22½ kg) of date syrup and put it in a vessel. Pour on it a similar amount of water and put it in a sunny place for 20 days. Take 5 *ratls* (5 lb/2¼ kg) of *dadhi* and a similar amount of honey. Put them in a cauldron and pour on them 10 *ratls* (20 cups/5 litres) of water. Boil them and then pour them into the prepared date syrup. Whip the mixture for three days after which you seal the vessel with mud. When two months have passed, open up the vessel. The wine will be splendid. (my translation)

Sauce for Boiled Ostrich: A Roman Recipe
— from *Apicius*, a cookery book from classical antiquity (*Apicius*, trans. C. Grocock and S. Grainger, Totnes, 2006)

Pepper, mint, roasted cumin, celery seed, long or round dates, honey, vinegar, *passum* [raisin wine], *liquamen* [fish sauce] and a little oil. Put in a pan and bring to the boil. Thicken it with starch and in this state pour over the pieces of ostrich on a serving dish and sprinkle with pepper. If, however, you want to cook [the ostrich] in the sauce then add *alica* [emmer groats].

Modern Recipes

Festive Stuffed Dates

A delicious recipe I learned from my mother.

20 pitted dates
20 toasted almonds or walnut halves
¼ cup (60 g) butter
1 cup (115 g) all-purpose/plain flour
¼ teaspoon ground cardamom

½ cup (125 ml) honey
For garnish: ground nuts of your choice

Stuff pitted dates with toasted nuts. In a small frying pan melt butter, and add flour. Stir all the time until flour is fragrant and evenly browned, about 5 minutes. Add cardamom.

Warm up honey to loosen its texture. Dip each filled date in it, and then roll it in the toasted flour immediately. Let the dates pick as much as possible of the flour. Spread the remaining flour on a dish and arrange dates on this bed. Sprinkle with ground nuts and serve with coffee.

Date Sweetmeat for People on the Go

An easy recipe, popular in the Arab world today. In medieval times, it was called *hays*, made of date paste combined with crushed *ka'k*, which is a dry variety of cookie/biscuit, and enhanced with clarified butter. It was part of the Arab travellers' victuals because it kept very well. Interestingly, for some pre-Islamic Arab tribes, it had a rather peculiar use. It was made into idols, which they worshipped and – when pressed by hunger – they ate, without having any qualms. Think of all the flies that such gods might have attracted while still 'in business'! I wonder if there is any connection between such practices and the worship of Beelzebub, 'Lord of the Flies'.

¼ cup (60 g) butter
2 cups (350 g) pitted chopped dates
½ cup (60 g) crushed *ka'k* (may be replaced with graham
crackers or digestive biscuits)
½ teaspoon each of ground cardamom, fennel and coriander
seeds
½ cup (60 g) nuts of your choice

In a heavy duty frying pan, melt butter on medium heat. Add dates, and mix and mash with the back of a spoon. If dates are a bit dry and hard to mash, add a little hot water to soften them.

While mashing, gradually sprinkle in the crushed graham crackers, cardamom, fennel and coriander (total time 7 to 10 minutes). Then spread the mixture on a flat tray or plate, about ½ inch (1 cm) thick. Press the nuts well on the entire surface. When cool enough, cut into squares and serve.

Date Shake

A simple shake adapted from Oasis Date Gardens website, www. oasisdategardens.com, where you may find many interesting date recipes. Another online resource for an astonishing number of creations with dates is www.datesaregreat.com, of The California Date Administrative Committee.

½ cup (90 g) chopped dried dates
½ cup (125 ml) milk
3 scoops vanilla ice cream
flavouring of your choice

Puree dates and milk in a blender, then add ice cream, and mix until smooth. You may flavour the shake with a bit of rose water, ground cardamom or cinnamon. Top the shake with pieces of chopped dates and nuts, or drizzle with a bit of chocolate sauce.

Date Chutney
(Makes about 4 cups/1 litre)

½ cup (125 ml) wine vinegar
½ cup (125 ml) orange juice
½ cup (125 ml) water
¼ cup (60 ml) oil
¼ cup (60 ml) honey
1 cup (225 g) granulated sugar
1 cup (180 g) chopped dried dates
1 cup (180 g) dried apricots

1 medium onion, cut in half and thinly sliced
1 garlic clove, crushed
4 chopped fresh chillies, or crushed dried ones
1 teaspoon ground nutmeg
1 teaspoon coriander seeds
1 teaspoon cumin
1 teaspoon ginger
1 teaspoon salt

Put all the ingredients in a medium heavy pot. Bring to the boil quickly, stirring to help sugar dissolve, about 10 minutes. Reduce heat to low, and let the mix simmer until it thickens nicely, about 40 minutes.

Cupid's Omelet
(Serves 2)

A traditional Middle Eastern dish, believed to be aphrodisiac, especially if served with a small glass of milk or carrot juice.

½ cup (90 g) chopped dried dates
2 tablespoons butter
3 eggs, slightly beaten
salt and black pepper

Put dates and butter in a medium frying pan, and stir on medium heat, until dates soften and emit a nice caramelized aroma. Pour the eggs all over and carefully fold until the eggs are set. Sprinkle with salt and pepper. A sprinkle of cinnamon will be good, too. Share the dish with your significant other and plan on having the house for yourselves.

Braised Chicken with Nuts and Dates
(Serves 4)

FOR THE CHICKEN
4 chicken thighs or 8 drumsticks
1 teaspoon salt
½ teaspoon black pepper
3 tablespoons all-purpose/plain flour
3 tablespoons oil

1 medium onion, coarsely chopped
1 cup (180 g) dried dates, quartered
2 cups (475 ml) water
½ cup (55 g) ground walnuts
2 tablespoons lemon juice
1 teaspoon crushed coriander seeds
½ teaspoon salt
¼ teaspoon black pepper

Sprinkle thighs or drumsticks with salt and pepper, then coat with flour, and quickly brown on both sides in heated oil in a large non-stick frying pan, about 10 minutes. Transfer chicken to a plate. In the remaining oil, sauté onion until transparent, about 5 minutes. Then add the dates, and stir for a minute. Add water, walnuts, lemon juice, coriander seeds, salt, and pepper. Bring to the boil quickly, stirring occasionally, about 5 minutes.

Return chicken to frying pan, arrange in one layer, cover with a lid (or kitchen foil), and let simmer about 30 minutes, or until chicken is tender and sauce is nicely thickened. Garnish with chopped parsley and serve with steamed rice or couscous.

Fried Fish with Date Sauce
(Serves 4)

1 tablespoon oil
1 medium onion, coarsely chopped
1 teaspoon curry powder
2 cloves garlic, thinly sliced
¾ cup (135 g) chopped dates
1 tablespoon pomegranate syrup or Worcestershire sauce
1 teaspoon crushed coriander seeds
1 teaspoon salt
¼ teaspoon black pepper
½ cup (125 ml) water
4 serving-size pieces of fish fillet of your choice, fried
4 servings of steamed white rice

In a medium frying pan, sauté onion in oil until translucent, about 5 minutes. Stir in curry powder in the last 30 seconds. Add the rest of the ingredients, except for fish and rice, and stir and cook until sauce nicely thickens (about 10 minutes). Fry the fish. On a large platter, spread the rice, arrange the fish pieces all over and top with the date sauce.

Date-Filled Cookies/Biscuits

Traditional pastries, called *kleicha* in Iraq and *ma'moul* in the rest of the Arab world. Similar ones, called *qullupu*, were made in ancient Mesopotamia, and in medieval Islam they were called *khushkanaj*.

FOR THE COOKIE/BISCUIT DOUGH
3 cups (350 g) all-purpose/plain flour
1 tablespoon sugar
½ teaspoon baking powder
½ teaspoon cardamom
½ teaspoon ground aniseed

¼ teaspoon cinnamon
¼ teaspoon crushed nigella seeds
¼ teaspoon salt
¾ cup (180 ml) oil or melted butter
⅔ cup (160 ml) water
1 egg, slightly beaten for glaze

FOR THE FILLING
2 cups (350 g) pitted dates
About ¼ cup (60 ml) water
2 tablespoons butter
½ teaspoon ground cinnamon, cardamom, coriander seeds,
each
¼ cup (30 g) toasted sesame seeds
1 teaspoon rose water or orange blossom water

Preheat oven to 400°F/200°C. In a big bowl, combine all the dry ingredients of the dough. Pour in the oil or butter, and rub the mixture between your fingers until it resembles breadcrumbs. Add water, and stir in a circular movement to incorporate liquid into flour. Then knead for about 5 minutes to form pliable dough of medium consistency.

To make the filling, put the dates, water and butter in a heavy frying pan. Cook over low heat mashing dates with the back of a spoon until they soften. Add the rest of the ingredients, and mix well.

To shape the cookies, take a piece of dough the size of a walnut and flatten it with the fingers into a disc. Put a heaping teaspoon of date filling in the middle of the disc. Gather the edges and seal them well to prevent date from showing. Put the stuffed piece into the concave of the wooden *ma'moul* mould (available at Middle Eastern stores), press it well and tap it out, and repeat with the rest. Arrange cookies on a baking sheet, brush them with beaten egg, and bake them in the preheated oven until golden brown, 15 to 20 minutes.

Spicy Date Cake

1½ cups (285 g) whole seedless dates
1¼ cups (310 ml) brewed tea
½ cup (125 ml) oil (such as canola)
1½ cups (350 g) granulated sugar
3 eggs
1½ teaspoons vanilla
2½ cups (250 g) all-purpose/plain flour
2 teaspoons baking powder
½ teaspoon salt
1 teaspoon cinnamon
1 teaspoon cardamom
¼ teaspoon ground nutmeg
¼ teaspoon cloves
½ cup (60 g) walnuts, broken into small pieces

Preheat oven to 375°F/190°C. Put the dates and tea in a small pot. Bring to the boil quickly, then simmer for about 10 minutes, or until dates soften (but are not mushy). Drain the dates, but reserve the drained liquid. Let them cool off to room temperature. Cut the drained dates into small pieces, and add enough cold water to liquid to make it measure ⅔ cup (160 ml).

In a big bowl, put oil, sugar, eggs and vanilla, and beat for 2 minutes. Sift together the flour, baking powder, salt and spices. Stir the flour mix into the egg mix in two batches, alternately with the measured date liquid. Stir in the walnuts and dates. Divide the batter between two 9 in./23 cm round baking pans. Bake for 40 minutes, or until surface feels firm to the touch. Let them stand for 10 minutes and then invert on a cooling rack.

When completely cool, divide the cakes into halves, and fill the layers with whipped heavy/double cream, delicately sweetened with confectioners'/icing sugar, and flavoured with rose water. Do not put any cream on the face of the cake. Instead, cover it with the following glaze:

½ cup (115 g) packed, brown/soft brown sugar
¼ cup (60 ml) heavy/double cream
3 tablespoons butter
½ cup (85 g) confectioners'/icing sugar, sifted
1 teaspoon vanilla

In a small saucepan, combine sugar, cream and butter. Bring to the boil, on medium heat, stirring to allow sugar to dissolve. Boil gently for about 2 minutes. Let it cool off to room temperature. Stir in the icing sugar and add vanilla, until smooth. It should be neither too thick nor too runny in consistency. Use immediately.

References

Introducing the Date

1 Pliny the Elder, *Natural History*, Book XIII, chap. 9.
2 Ibid., Book XIII, chap. 9.
3 W. F. Wigston, *Bacon, Shakespeare, and the Rosicrucians* (London, 1884), p. 96.
4 Kelli Burton, 'Methuselah Tree Grows from Ages-Old Seed', *Boston Globe* (16 June 2008), pp. C1–2.
5 The Arabic *deqel* gradually developed a more specialized sense: date palm grown from a seedling, whose parentage is unknown.
6 Hehn Victor and James Mallory, *Cultivated Plants and Domesticated Animals in their Migration from Asia to Europe: Historico-Linguistic Studies* (Amsterdam, 1976), p. 208.
7 E. Corner, *Natural History of Palms* (Berkeley and Los Angeles, 1966), p. 1.

1 Looking After the Date

1 P. B. Popenoe and Charles Bennett, *Date Growing in the Old World and the New: With a Chapter on the Food Value of the Date* (Altadena, CA, 1913), p. 249.
2 Ibn Wahshiyya, *Al-Filaha al-Nabatiyya* (Nabatean agriculture), ed. Tawfiq Fahd (Damascus, 1995), vol. II, p. 1406.

3 George Contenau, *Everyday Life in Babylon and Assyria* (London, 1954), p. 255.

4 Herodotus, *The Histories*, Book I, Section 193

5 Pliny the Elder, *Natural History*, Book XIII, chap. 7.

6 V.H.W. Dowson and A. Aten, *Dates: Handling, Processing, and Packing* (Rome, 1962), pp. 68–9.

7 Ibid., p. 217.

8 Pliny, *Natural History*, Book XIII, chap. 7.

2 Date Varieties

1 Pliny the Elder, *Natural History*, Book XIII, chap. 9.

2 Al-Biruni (d. 1048), *Kitab Al-Saydana* (Book of pharmacy), ed. and trans. Hakim Muhammad Sa'id (Karachi, 1973), p. 117.

3 Xenophon, *Anabasis*, Book II, chap. 3.

4 P. B. Popenoe and Charles Bennett, *Date Growing in the Old World and the New: With a Chapter on the Food Value of the Date* (Altadena, CA, 1913), p. 228.

5 Ibid., pp. 260–61.

6 Ibid., p. 261.

7 The most extensive list descriptive of date varieties is in Popenoe and Bennett's book on dates, *Date Growing in the Old World and the New*, (Part II: 'Date Varieties', pp. 209–97).

8 Eric Hansen, 'Looking for the Khalasah', *Saudi Aramco World* (July/August 2004), p. 3.

3 The 360 Uses of the Date Palm

1 James Pritchard, *The Ancient Near East* (New Jersey, 1975), vol. II, pp. 142–5.

2 *Geography of Strabo*, Volume III, Book XVI, Chapter 1, Section 14.

3 Henri Limet, 'The Cuisine of Ancient Sumer', *Biblical Archaeologist*, I/3 (September 1987), pp. 133–4; Hilary

Wilson, *Egyptian Food and Drink* (Buckinghamshire, 2001),
p. 18.
4 Pliny the Elder, *Natural History*, Book XIV, chap. 19.
5 Qur'an, Sura 19, verse 26.
6 S. Langdon, *Tammuz and Ishtar: A Monograph upon Babylonian Religion and Theology* (Oxford, 1914), p. 59.
7 Ibid., p. 62.
8 Qur'an, Sura 19, verse 23.
9 Campbell Thompson, *A Dictionary of Assyrian Botany* (London, 1949), pp. 308–11.

4 The Eminent History of the Date

1 George Contenau, *Everyday Life in Babylon and Assyria* (London, 1954), p. 292.
2 The Electronic Text Corpus of Sumerian Literature, at www-etcsl.orient.ox.ac.uk [accessed 7 May 2010].
3 C. Scott Littleton, ed., *Mythology* (London, 2002), p. 626.
4 Old Testament, 1 Kings, 6: 29, 32, 35; 7: 36.
5 Psalm 92: 12.
6 Solomon 7: 6–8.
7 Genesis 2: 9.
8 Revelation 22: 2.
9 W. F. Wigston, *Bacon, Shakespeare, and the Rosicrucians* (London, 1884), p. 97.
10 Cited by Hehn Victor and James Mallory, *Cultivated Plants and Domesticated Animals in their Migration from Asia to Europe: Historico-Linguistic Studies* (Amsterdam, 1976), p. 204.
11 Bedowee is 'bedouin'; Nejidee, a horse of excellent breed; Almeh, 'Egyptian professional entertainer'. Poem cited by Samuel Zwemer, *Arabia: The Cradle of Islam* (London, 1900), pp. 121–2.
12 At www.roadsideamerica.com [accessed 7 May 2010].

5 Looking for the Date: A Bird's Eye View

1 D. Milne, *The Date Palm and its Cultivation in the Punjab* (Lyallpur, 1918), p. 154.
2 Marc Beech, 'Archaeological Evidence for Early Date Consumption in the Arabian Gulf', in *The Date Palm: From Traditional Resource to Green Wealth* (Abu Dhabi, 2003), p. 18.
3 Theophrastus, *Enquiry into Plants*, vol. 11, Book 6.
4 Pliny the Elder, *Natural History*, Book XIII, chaps 6–9.
5 Daniel Potts, 'Date Palms and Date Consumption in Eastern Arabia during the Bronze Age', in *The Date Palm: From Traditional Resource to Green Wealth*, p. 45.
6 Justus Doolittle, ed., *From the Chinese Recorder and Missionary Journal* (Foochow, 1871), XXII, pp. 265–6.
7 At www.lastories.com [accessed 7 May 2010].
8 Hilda Simon, *The Date Palm: Bread of the Desert* (New York, 1978), pp. 83–4.
9 Ibid., p. 89.
10 'The Story of Dates', *Periscope* (Coachella Valley Historical Society, 2007), part II, p. 37.

6 The Future of the Date

1 Emmanuelle Landais, 'Dates Could Hold Future of Creating Local Biofuel', *Gulf News*, 2 October 2009.

Select Bibliography

Barreveld, W. H., *Date Palm Products* (Rome, 1993)

Clark, Arthur, 'Cake for the Poor', *Saudi Aramco World* (January/February 1985), pp. 2–7

Corner, E.J.H., *The Natural History of Palms* (Berkeley and Los Angeles, 1966)

The Date Palm: From Traditional Resource to Green Wealth, The Emirate Center for Strategic Studies and Research (Abu Dhabi, 2003)

Dowson, V.H.W. and A. Aten, *Dates: Handling, Processing, and Packing* (Rome, 1962)

Hansen, Eric, 'Carrying Dates to Hajar', *Saudi Aramco World* (July/August 2004), pp. 9–8

—, 'Looking for the Khalasah', *Saudi Aramco World* (July/August 2004), pp. 2–8

Heetland, Rick, *Date Recipes* (Phoenix, AZ, 1993)

Laflin, Patricia, 'The Story of Dates', *Periscope* (Coachella Valley Historical Society, 2006–7)

Lunde, Paul, 'A History of Dates', *Saudi Aramco World* (March/April 1978), pp. 20–23

Milne, D., *The Date Palm and its Cultivation in the Punjab* (Lyallpur, 1918)

Morton, Julia, 'Date', in *Fruits of Warm Climates* (Miami, 1987), pp. 5–11

Paulsen, Marc, *The Amazing Story of the Fabulous Medjool Date* (Bard, CA, 2008)

Popenoe, P. B. and Charles Bennett, *Date Growing in the Old World and the New: With a Chapter on the Food Value of the Date* (Altadena, CA, 1913)

Potts, Daniel, *Feast of Dates* (Abu Dhabi, 2002)

Simon, Hilda, *The Date Palm: Bread of the Desert* (New York, 1978)

Swingle, W. T., *The Date Palm and its Utilization in the Southwestern States* (Washington, DC, 1904)

Zaid, Abdelouahhab, ed., *Date Palm Cultivation* (Rome, 2002)

Websites and Associations

California Dates
www.datesaregreat.com

Date Palm Global Network
http://dpgn.uaeu.ac.ae

The Food Museum Online
www.foodmuseum.com/datepalm.html

Oasis Date Gardens
www.oasisdategardens.com

Palm Wonder, Saudi Arabia
www.palmwonders.com

Shields Date Garden
http://shieldsdates.com

Acknowledgements

The seed of this book was a talk I gave to the Culinary Historians of New York a couple of years ago. At the suggestion of Cathy Kaufman, President of the group, I expanded the scope of the subject to cover dates in general. Among the audience was Michael Leaman, publisher of Reaktion Books, and Andrew Smith, editor of the Edible Series, who saw in it a potential for a book for their series. I am deeply indebted to them all.

Along the road of writing it, a lot of dates were devoured and kindnesses encountered. I would like to thank the obliging staffs of museums and institutions who made the experience of obtaining images pleasurable. Betsy Kohut of the Smithsonian Institution was as helpful as ever. I am grateful to the staff of *Saudi Aramco World* as well as Georg Popp and Michael Dickenson of Arabia Felix Synform GmbH, for generously allowing me to scoop from their rich archives. My thanks extend to Bernadette Simpson for her beautiful palm image, and Patricia Laflin, date historian of the Coachella Valley Historical Society, for her informative and pleasant phone exchanges. I am also grateful to the Iraqi artist Maysaloon Faraj for generously offering many of her moving paintings to choose from, and to her namesake Maysaloon Hadi, Iraqi novelist and friend, for introducing me to her.

I am blissfully overwhelmed by the constant support and enthusiasm of family and friends, whose love for dates has been inspirational. My warmest gratitude belongs to Shakir, whose gift for our thirtieth wedding anniversary was a memorable trip to Coachella Valley in California, where it felt like home away from home.

Photo Acknowledgements

The author and publishers wish to express their thanks to the following sources of illustrative material and/or permission to reproduce it:

© The Trustees of the British Museum: pp. 71 (IFF 10 - 133043), 76 (BM. 89132), 94 (BM. 5396); © Brooklyn Museum: (05.14) p. 82; photo George & Audrey DeLange: p. 36; © Museum of Fine Arts Boston, Charles Amos Cummings Fund and Gift of Horace L. Mayer: (60.133) p. 30; painting courtesy of Maysaloun Faraj: p. 97; Harvard Art Museum, Arthur M. Sackler Museum, Loan from the Trustees of the Arthur Stone Dewing Greek Numismatic Foundation (1.195.987)/ Photo Imaging Department © President and Fellows of Harvard College: p. 12; photo Hirmer Verlag GmbH, Munich, Hethiter (602.0816): p. 72; photos Frank Hurley, National Library of Australia: pp. 28 (NLA.PIC-AN23564759), 61 (NLA.PIC-AN23664812), 101 (NLA.PIC-AN24164777); sketch Austin Layard, Monuments of Nineveh, p. 78; photos Nawal Nasrallah: pp. 6, 13, 15, 20, 21, 22, 24 (bottom), 25, 29, 34, 35, 37, 40 (bottom), 42, 44, 58, 64, 68, 70, 86, 89, 91, 96, 103, 105, 109, 110; photo Palm Springs Historical Society: p. 41; photos courtesy of Georg Popp www.oman-archive.com: pp. 10, 24 (top), 46, 53, 63, 98; photos courtesy of © Saudi Aramco/SAWDIA: pp. 90 (Eric Hansen), 31, 33, 55 (John Feeney) 39 (Arthur Clark) 43, 83 (Khalil Abou El-Nasr) 62 (Michael Di Biase) 99; photo courtesy of Bernadette Simpson: pp. 9, 40 (top); © Smithsonian Freer Gallery of Art and Arthur M. Sackler Gallery: pp. (F1908.268) 17 (F1954.81), 49; Stock xchng: p. 8 (Lucyna Andrzejewka); © Topkapi Palace Museum (H.761, 133b): pp. 18, 88.

Index

italic numbers refer to illustrations; **bold** to recipes